CAMBRIDGE
UNIVERSITY PRESS

Biology

for Cambridge IGCSE™

WORKBOOK

Mary Jones & Geoff Jones

CAMBRIDGE
UNIVERSITY PRESS

University Printing House, Cambridge CB2 8BS, United Kingdom

One Liberty Plaza, 20th Floor, New York, NY 10006, USA

477 Williamstown Road, Port Melbourne, VIC 3207, Australia

314–321, 3rd Floor, Plot 3, Splendor Forum, Jasola District Centre, New Delhi – 110025, India

103 Penang Road, #05-06/07, Visioncrest Commercial, Singapore 238467

Cambridge University Press is part of the University of Cambridge.

It furthers the University's mission by disseminating knowledge in the pursuit of education, learning and research at the highest international levels of excellence.

www.cambridge.org
Information on this title: www.cambridge.org/9781108947480

© Cambridge University Press 2021

Second edition 2009
Third edition 2014
Fourth edition 2021

20 19 18 17 16 15 14 13 12 11 10 9 8 7 6

Printed in Italy by Rotolito S.p.A.

A catalogue record for this publication is available from the British Library

ISBN 978-1-108-94748-0 Workbook with Digital Access (2 Years)

Additional resources for this publication at www.cambridge.org/go

Illustrations by Eleanor Jones

DEDICATED TEACHER AWARDS

Teachers play an important part in shaping futures. Our Dedicated Teacher Awards recognise the hard work that teachers put in every day.

Thank you to everyone who nominated this year; we have been inspired and moved by all of your stories. Well done to all of our nominees for your dedication to learning and for inspiring the next generation of thinkers, leaders and innovators.

Congratulations to our incredible winner and finalists!

WINNER

Patricia Abril
New Cambridge School,
Colombia

Stanley Manaay
Salvacion National High School,
Philippines

Tiffany Cavanagh
Trident College Solwezi,
Zambia

Helen Comerford
Lumen Christi Catholic College,
Australia

John Nicko Coyoca
University of San Jose-Recoletos,
Philippines

Meera Rangarajan
RBK International Academy,
India

For more information about our dedicated teachers and their stories, go to
dedicatedteacher.cambridge.org

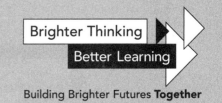

Brighter Thinking
Better Learning

Building Brighter Futures **Together**

> Contents

> How to use this series

We offer a comprehensive, flexible array of resources for the Cambridge IGCSE™ Biology syllabus. We provide targeted support and practice for the specific challenges we've heard that students face: learning science with English as a second language; learners who find the mathematical content within science difficult; and developing practical skills.

The coursebook provides coverage of the full Cambridge IGCSE Biology syllabus. Each chapter explains facts and concepts, and uses relevant real-world examples of scientific principles to bring the subject to life. Together with a focus on practical work and plenty of active learning opportunities, the coursebook prepares learners for all aspects of their scientific study. At the end of each chapter, examination-style questions offer practice opportunities for learners to apply their learning.

The digital teacher's resource contains detailed guidance for all topics of the syllabus, including common misconceptions identifying areas where learners might need extra support, as well as an engaging bank of lesson ideas for each syllabus topic. Differentiation is emphasised with advice for identification of different learner needs and suggestions of appropriate interventions to support and stretch learners. The teacher's resource also contains support for preparing and carrying out all the investigations in the practical workbook, including a set of sample results for when practicals aren't possible.

The teacher's resource also contains scaffolded worksheets and unit tests for each chapter. Answers for all components are accessible to teachers for free on the Cambridge GO platform.

The skills-focused workbook has been carefully constructed to help learners develop the skills that they need as they progress through their Cambridge IGCSE Biology course, providing further practice of all the topics in the coursebook. A three-tier, scaffolded approach to skills development enables students to gradually progress through 'focus', 'practice' and 'challenge' exercises, ensuring that every learner is supported. The workbook enables independent learning and is ideal for use in class or as homework.

The practical workbook provides learners additional opportunities for hands-on practical work, giving them full guidance and support that will help them to develop their investigative skills. These skills include planning investigations, selecting and handling apparatus, creating hypotheses, recording and displaying results, and analysing and evaluating data.

Mathematics is an integral part of scientific study, and one that learners often find a barrier to progression in science. The Maths Skills for Cambridge IGCSE Biology write-in workbook has been written in collaboration with the Association of Science Education, with each chapter focusing on several maths skills that students need to succeed in their Biology course.

Our research shows that English language skills are the single biggest barrier to students accessing international science. This write-in English language skills workbook contains exercises set within the context of IGCSE Biology topics to consolidate understanding and embed practice in aspects of language central to the subject. Activities range from practising using 'effect' and 'affect' in the context of enzymes, to writing about expiration with a focus on common prefixes.

> How to use this book

Throughout this book, you will notice lots of different features that will help your learning. These are explained below. Answers are accessible to teachers for free on the 'supporting resources' area of the Cambridge GO website.

KEY WORDS

Definitions for useful vocabulary are given at the start of each section. You will also find definitions for these words in the Glossary at the back of this book.

Supplement content: In the key word boxes, Supplement content is indicated with a large arrow, as in this example.

LEARNING INTENTIONS

These set the scene for each exercise, beginning with 'In this exercise you will:', and indicate the important concepts.

> In the learning intentions box, Supplement content is indicated with a large arrow and a darker background, as in this example.

TIPS

The information in these boxes will help you complete the exercises, and give you support in areas that you might find difficult.

Exercises

These help you to practise skills that are important for studying IGCSE Biology.

Questions within exercises fall into one of three types:

- Focus questions will help build your basic skills.
- Practice questions provide more opportunities for practice, pushing your skills further.
- Challenge questions will stretch and challenge you even further.

SELF/PEER ASSESSMENT

At the end of some exercises, you will find opportunities to help you assess your own work, or that of your classmates, and consider how you can improve the way you learn.

> Supplement content

Where content is intended for students who are studying the Supplement content of the syllabus as well as the Core, this is indicated with the arrow and the bar, as you can see on the left here.

> Introduction

This Cambridge IGCSE™ Biology workbook has been written to help you develop the skills you need for your course for Cambridge IGCSE Biology (0610/0970). To succeed in this course, you need to have an excellent factual knowledge of all the topics in the syllabus and you also need to be able to think like a scientist. As you work through the book, chapter by chapter, you will develop the relevant scientific skills needed and gain the confidence to use them yourself. The exercises in this workbook provide opportunities for you to practise the following skills:

- finding information in text, diagrams or graphs, and then using it to answer questions

- changing information in one form into another form – for example, using words to describe a graph, or a diagram to summarise some text

- using technical vocabulary correctly

- doing calculations, showing your working clearly

- using information to identify patterns and/or trends, and making inferences

- suggesting explanations for unfamiliar data or other information provided, using your understanding of the biology you have learnt in your course

- making suitable predictions or hypotheses

- solving problems relating to biology topics

- planning and evaluating experiments.

The exercises in each chapter will help you develop these skills by applying them to new contexts. The chapters are arranged in the same order as the chapters in the Cambridge IGCSE Biology coursebook. Each exercise has an introduction that outlines the skills you will be developing.

We hope that this book will help you succeed in your Cambridge IGCSE Biology course, give you the necessary scientific skills to help you with your future studies, and inspire you to have a love of biological science.

This workbook is designed to support the Cambridge IGCSE Biology coursebook, with specially selected topics where students would benefit from further opportunities to apply skills, such as application, analysis and evaluation, in addition to developing knowledge and understanding.

Chapter 1

Characteristics and classification of living organisms

> Characteristics of living organisms

KEY WORDS

excretion: the removal of the waste products of metabolism and substances in excess of requirements

growth: a permanent increase in size and dry mass

metabolic reactions: chemical reactions that take place in living organisms

movement: an action by an organism or part of an organism causing a change of position or place

nutrition: taking in materials for energy, growth and development

organism: a living thing

reproduction: the processes that make more of the same kind of organism

respiration: the chemical reactions in cells that break down nutrient molecules and release energy for metabolism

sensitivity: the ability to detect and respond to changes in the internal or external environment

Exercise 1.1

IN THIS EXERCISE YOU WILL:

practise naming and describing the characteristics of living things.

Focus

1   Draw lines to match each term with its description.

Term	Description

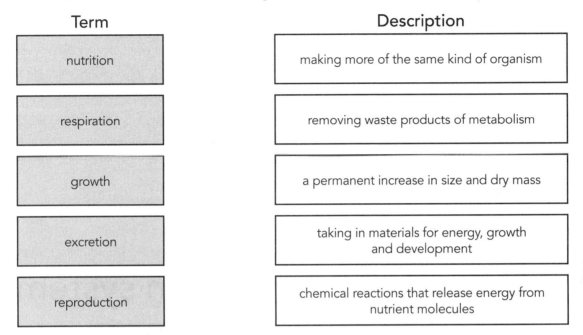

Term:
- nutrition
- respiration
- growth
- excretion
- reproduction

Description:
- making more of the same kind of organism
- removing waste products of metabolism
- a permanent increase in size and dry mass
- taking in materials for energy, growth and development
- chemical reactions that release energy from nutrient molecules

Practice

2   Figure 1.1 shows a plant, growing towards the light. Inside its leaves, photosynthesis is taking place. Photosynthesis uses carbon dioxide to make glucose, and releases oxygen.

Add labels to Figure 1.1. Your labels should include short descriptions stating how the plant is showing these characteristics of living things:

- reproduction
- growth
- sensitivity
- excretion

Figure 1.1: A plant growing towards the light.

Challenge

3 Imagine that someone from another planet is visiting Earth. They see aeroplanes and birds moving through the sky.

Explain to the visitor why birds are alive and aeroplanes are not alive, even though they seem to share some of the characteristics of living things.

....

....

....

....

....

....

> The biological classification system

KEY WORDS

binomial system: a system of naming species that is internationally agreed, in which the scientific name is made up of two parts showing the genus and the species

fertile: able to reproduce

genus: a group of species that share similar features and a common ancestor

species: a group of organisms that can reproduce to produce fertile offspring

Exercise 1.2

IN THIS EXERCISE YOU WILL:

• check that you know what a binomial is

• practise finding evidence in a short, written passage

• think about advantages of using the binomial system.

Focus

4 Complete the sentences, using words from the list.

binomial   biological   complete   fertile   genus   group   healthy

living   population   reproduce   species

An organism is a .... thing. A .... is a group of living organisms

that can .... with each other to produce .... offspring.

Each species of organism has a two-word name. This system of naming is called the

.... system. The first of the two words in the name tells us the ....

that the species belongs to.

Practice

5 Tigers, *Panthera tigris*, and lions, *Panthera leo*, sometimes mate with each other if they are kept together in a zoo. The offspring are called ligers. Ligers are perfectly healthy, but are unable to reproduce.

Use this information to write down:

a   *one* piece of evidence that lions and tigers are closely related

....

....

b   *two* pieces of evidence that lions and tigers belong to different species.

....

....

....

....

Challenge

6 Many people dislike using binomials for species. They would prefer to just use English names. Explain why it is helpful to scientists to use the binomial system.

....

....

....

....

> Keys

Exercise 1.3: Focus

IN THIS EXERCISE YOU WILL:

practise using a key to identify four animals.

7   Figure 1.2 shows four vertebrates.

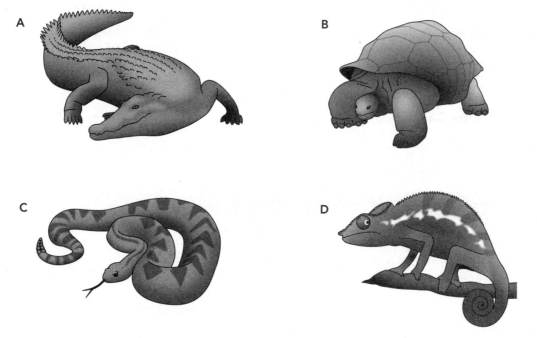

Figure 1.2: Four vertebrates.

Use the dichotomous key to identify each of these four animals.

List the sequence of statements that you worked through to find the name.

TIP

Remember to work on one animal at a time. Identify that one, then move on to the next.

1	**a**	shell present	*Geochelone elephantopus*
	b	shell absent	go to **2**
2	**a**	four legs	go to **3**
	b	no legs	*Ophiophagus hannah*
3	**a**	back and tail are covered with rough spikes	*Crocodylus niloticus*
	b	no spikes on tail	*Chamaeleo gracilis*

> **TIP**
>
> When writing binomials, underline them to show that they should be in italics. Remember that the genus name starts with a capital letter but the species name is all lowercase.

Animal A has been done for you.

A 1b, 2a, 3a – <u>Crocodylus niloticus</u> ....

B ....

C ....

D ....

Exercise 1.4: Practice

IN THIS EXERCISE YOU WILL:

practise writing a dichotomous key by completing one that has already been started.

8 Figure 1.3 shows a spider, locust, centipede and crab.

spider

locust

centipede

crab

Figure 1.3: Spider, locust, centipede and crab.

Here is the start of a key to help someone who does not know anything about these animals to identify them. Complete the key by writing more pairs of statements.

Then try your key out on a friend.

1 a has antennae .... go to **2**

  b does not have antennae .... spider

2 a has three pairs of legs ....

  b ....

3 a ....

  b ....

Exercise 1.5: Challenge

IN THIS EXERCISE YOU WILL:

write your own dichotomous key.

9 Figure 1.4 shows photographs of four species of fish.

Figure 1.4: Four species of fish.

Write a dichotomous key to enable someone to identify each of the four fish.

....

....

....

....

....

....

....

....

....

....

SELF-ASSESSMENT

How confident do you feel about using and writing keys? Rate yourself for each of the points in the checklist using:

🙂   if you did it really well

😐   if you made a good attempt at it and partly succeeded

🙁   if you did not try to do it, or did not succeed

Checklist	Rating
I can use a dichotomous key to identify organisms.	
I can complete a key that has already been started.	
I can write my own key with no help.	

What will you do to improve your ability to write a good dichotomous key?

....

....

....

> Kingdoms

KEY WORDS

fungus: an organism whose cells have cell walls, but that does not photosynthesise

hyphae: microscopic threads, made of cells linked in a long line, that make up the body of a fungus

kingdom: one of the major groups into which all organisms are classified

spores: very small groups of cells surrounded by a protective wall, used in reproduction

Exercise 1.6

IN THIS EXERCISE YOU WILL:

practise making the kind of drawing that is used in biology.

Biologists often need to describe clearly what they observe when studying organisms. One of the best ways to do this is to make a drawing.

A biological drawing needs to be simple, but clear. Sometimes, you need to label your drawing to indicate important features.

Here are some points to think about when you draw.

- Make good use of the space on your sheet of paper – your drawing should be large. However, do leave space around it so that you have room for labels.

- Always use a sharp HB pencil and have a good eraser with you.

- Keep all lines single and clear with no breaks.

- Do not use shading.

- Do not use colours.

- Take time to get the outline of your drawing correct first, showing the correct proportions. Do this lightly to start with, so that you can rub out and try again.

Here are some points to bear in mind when you label a diagram.

- Use a ruler to draw each label line.

- Make sure the end of the label line touches the structure being labelled.

- Write the labels horizontally.

- Keep the labels well away from the edges of your drawing.

- Do not let label lines cross one another.

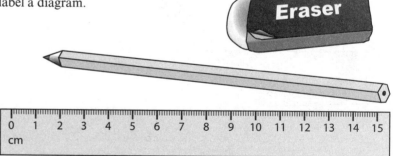

Focus

Figure 1.5 shows two drawings of a leaf made by learners.

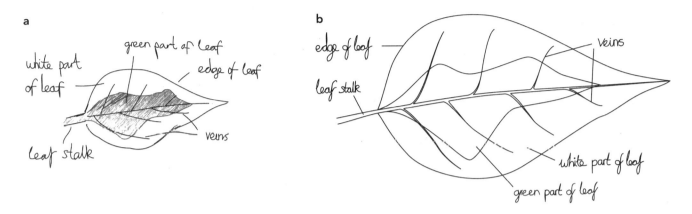

a

b

Figures 1.5 a and b: Two drawings of a leaf made by learners.

10   List *five* ways in which the second drawing (Figure 1.5b) is better than the first drawing (Figure 1.5a).

i   ....

ii ....

iii ....

iv ....

v   ....

Practice

11   Figure 1.6a is a photograph of an earthworm. A learner has begun to make a drawing of the earthworm (Figure 1.6b).

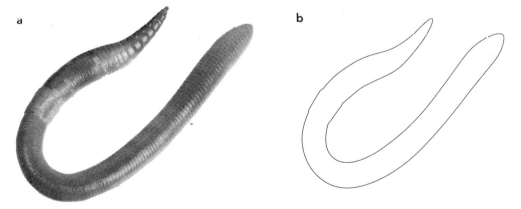

a

b

Figure 1.6 a: A photo of an earthworm. **b:** A drawing of the same earthworm.

a   Complete the drawing of the earthworm. Add *two* labels to your drawing.

b   Earthworms belong to the animal kingdom. Describe *two* features of an earthworm that you would *not* find in an organism belonging to the plant kingdom.

   i   ....

   ii ....

Challenge

12   Figure 1.7 is a photograph of a fungus.

Figure 1.7: A fungus, *Amanita muscaria*.

a   Draw a large diagram of the fungus in the space below. Do not label your diagram.

b Explain how organisms belonging to the fungus kingdom differ from those belonging to the plant kingdom.

....

....

....

....

....

....

....

....

SELF-ASSESSMENT

How confident do you feel about making a good biological drawing? Rate yourself for each of the points in the checklist using:

Green   if you did it really well

Amber   if you made a good attempt at it and partly succeeded

Red   if you did not try to do it, or did not succeed

Checklist	Colour
My drawing fills the space on the page, with enough room left for labels.	
I used a sharp pencil for the drawing.	
I did not use any shading or colours.	
All of the lines I drew are single and clear, with no breaks.	
The shape and proportions of my drawing are a good representation of the object.	

> Groups within the animal and plant kingdoms

> KEY WORDS

diaphragm: a muscle that separates the chest cavity from the abdominal cavity in mammals; it helps with breathing

dicotyledons: plants with two cotyledons in their seeds

exoskeleton: a supportive structure on the outside of the body

mammary glands: organs found only in mammals, which produce milk to feed young

metamorphosis: changing from a larva with one body form to an adult with a different body form

monocotyledons: plants with only one cotyledon in their seeds

pinna: a flap on the outside of the body that directs sound into the ear

placenta: an organ that connects the growing fetus to its mother, in which the blood of the fetus and mother are brought close together so that materials can be exchanged between them

Exercise 1.7: Focus

> IN THIS EXERCISE YOU WILL:

check that you remember the characteristic features of the five groups of vertebrates.

Table 1.1 shows some features of five vertebrates.

Animal	What is its skin like?	Does it have wings?	Does it have a beak?	What are its eggs like?
A	smooth	no	no	soft, without a shell
B	has hair	yes	no	does not lay eggs
C	has feathers	yes	yes	with a hard shell
D	has scales	no	no	soft, without a shell
E	has hair	no	no	does not lay eggs

Table 1.1: Features of five vertebrates.

13 Identify the group of vertebrates to which each animal belongs.

A ....   D ....

B ....   E ....

C ....

14 Animals **B** and **E** belong to the same group.

List *two* features of these animals, other than those in the table, that are characteristic features of this group.

i ....

ii ....

15 Name *one* group of vertebrates that is *not* included in the table.

....

Exercise 1.8: Practice

IN THIS EXERCISE YOU WILL:

practise remembering the characteristic features of the four groups of arthropods.

16 List *two* features that all arthropods share, that are *not* found in other groups in the animal kingdom.

i ....

ii ....

17 Complete the table to show the characteristic features of the four groups of arthropods.

Group	Number of pairs of legs	Number of pairs of antennae	Other distinguishing features, if any
arachnids			
insects			
myriapods			
crustaceans			

Exercise 1.9: Challenge

IN THIS EXERCISE YOU WILL:

practise remembering the characteristic features of ferns and flowering plants (monocotyledons and dicotyledons).

18 List *three* features shared by ferns and flowering plants, which are *not* shared by organisms in the animal or fungus kingdom.

i ....

ii ....

iii ....

19 Describe *two* ways in which ferns differ from flowering plants.

i ....

ii ....

20 Draw a table in the space below to summarise the characteristic features of monocotyledons and dicotyledons.

Chapter 2

Cells

› Animals, plants and bacteria

KEY WORDS

aerobic respiration: chemical reactions that take place in mitochondria, which use oxygen to break down glucose and other nutrient molecules to release energy for the cell to use

bacteria: unicellular organisms whose cells do not contain a nucleus

cell membrane: a very thin layer surrounding the cytoplasm of every cell; it controls what enters and leaves the cell

cell sap: the fluid that fills the large vacuoles in plant cells

cell wall: a tough layer outside the cell membrane; found in the cells of plants, fungi and bacteria

cells: the smallest units from which all organisms are made

cellulose: a carbohydrate that forms long fibres, and makes up the cell walls of plants

chromosome: a length of DNA, found in the nucleus of a cell; it contains genetic information in the form of many different genes

cytoplasm: the jelly-like material that fills a cell

DNA: a molecule that contains genetic information, in the form of genes, that controls the proteins that are made in the cell

fully permeable: allows all molecules and ions to pass through it

mitochondrion: a small structure in a cell, where aerobic respiration releases energy from glucose

nucleus: a structure containing DNA in the form of chromosomes

partially permeable: allows some molecules and ions to pass through, but not others

ribosomes: very small structures in a cell that use information on DNA to make protein molecules

vacuole: a fluid-filled space inside a cell, separated from the cytoplasm by a membrane

Exercise 2.1

IN THIS EXERCISE YOU WILL:

- practise drawing and labelling animal and plant cells
- outline the functions of some of the parts of cells
- use information to explain some of the features of a specialised cell.

Focus

Figure 2.1 shows an animal cell and the outline of a plant cell.

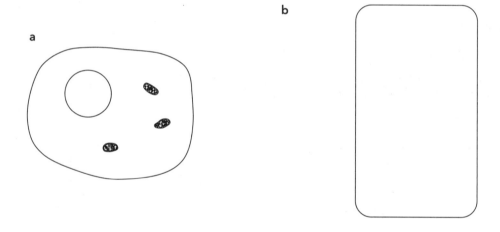

Figure 2.1 a: An animal cell. **b:** A plant cell.

1   On the animal cell diagram, label these parts:

   cell membrane   cytoplasm   mitochondrion   nucleus

2   Complete the diagram of the plant cell, and then label these parts:

   cell membrane   cell wall   chloroplast   cytoplasm   vacuole containing cell sap

   membrane around vacuole   mitochondrion   nucleus

SELF-ASSESSMENT

How confident do you feel about drawing a plant cell? Give yourself a mark for each of the points in the checklist. Award yourself:

2 marks if you did it well

1 mark if you made a good attempt at it and partly succeeded

0 marks if you did not try to do it, or did not succeed

Checklist	Marks awarded
I used a sharp pencil for drawing.	
I drew single clean lines; the lines are not broken or fuzzy.	
I did not use any shading or colours.	
I drew the parts of the cell in the right place (check against Figure 2.3, Chapter 2 in the Coursebook).	
I drew label lines with a ruler.	
Each label line touches the part it is labelling.	
Total (out of 12):	

Practice

3 Describe the function of each of these parts in a plant cell.

cell membrane

....

....

mitochondrion

....

....

chloroplast

....

....

4 Describe the function of each of these parts in a bacterial cell.

cell wall

....

....

ribosome

....

....

circular DNA

....

....

Challenge

5 Neurones are cells that transmit electrical signals throughout the body. This requires a lot of energy. They also synthesise (make) proteins, which help them to communicate with other neurones nearby.

Use this information to explain why neurones contain many mitochondria and many ribosomes.

....

....

....

....

....

....

> Specialised cells and sizes of specimens

Exercise 2.2

IN THIS EXERCISE YOU WILL:

- use the magnification equation

- practise giving answers to a required number of decimal places

- practise rearranging the magnification equation

> convert from millimetres to micrometres (µm) when using the magnification equation.

Focus

6   Complete the equation that we can use to calculate magnification.

magnification =

7   An apple is 60 mm in diameter. In a photograph of the apple, the apple is 120 mm in diameter. What is the magnification of the photograph? Show your working.

×....................

8   Figure 2.2 shows a leaf.

Figure 2.2: A leaf.

The actual length of the leaf is 32 mm.

a Measure the length of the leaf in Figure 2.2. Write down your answer.

....

> **TIP**
>
> It is always best to measure in millimetres (mm). Remember to write the unit when you write down your measurement.

b Calculate the magnification of the leaf image in Figure 2.2.

Show your working. Give your answer to one decimal place.

×...................

Practice

9 Look at the diagram of animal **D** in Chapter 1, Figure 1.2.

a Measure the length of animal **D** from its nose to the base of its tail.

....

b The actual length of this animal is 105 mm.

Calculate the magnification of the diagram.

Show your working and give your answer to two decimal places.

×...................

> **TIP**
>
> If an object is drawn smaller than its actual size, then the magnification is less than 1.

10 A photograph of an ant shows the length of the ant's antennae is 25 mm long.
The magnification of the photograph is ×12.

Calculate the actual size of the ant's antennae. Show your working and give your answer in millimetres, to the nearest whole number.

....

Challenge

11 Figure 2.3 shows a specialised cell.

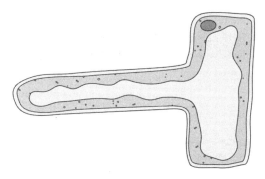

Figure 2.3: A specialised cell.

a   Name this cell *and* describe its function.

   ....

   ....

   ....

b   An actual root hair cell is about 100 μm long.

   Calculate the magnification of the diagram. Show your working. Give your answer to three significant figures.

                                                        ×....................

Movement into and out of cells

> Diffusion

Exercise 3.1

IN THIS EXERCISE YOU WILL:

- calculate means, to complete a results chart
- decide whether a set of results support a hypothesis
- think about the design of an experiment, including standardising variables
- identify sources of error and suggest improvements.

A learner did an experiment to test this hypothesis:

The higher the temperature, the faster diffusion takes place.

She took four Petri dishes containing agar jelly. She cut four holes in the jelly in each dish.

She placed $0.5\,cm^3$ of a solution containing a red dye (coloured substance) into each hole.

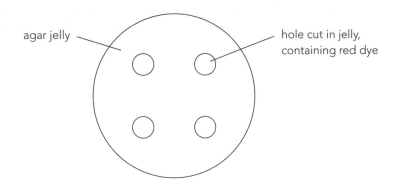

agar jelly

hole cut in jelly,
containing red dye

Figure 3.1: Petri dish of agar jelly with four holes.

The learner then covered the dishes and carefully placed them in different temperatures.
She left them for two hours. Then she measured how far the red dye had diffused into the agar
around each hole.

Table 3.1 shows the learner's results.

| Dish | Temperature / °C | Distance red dye had diffused into the jelly / mm | | | | |
		Hole 1	Hole 2	Hole 3	Hole 4	Mean (average)
A	10	2	3	2	3	
B	20	5	5	6	4	
C	40	9	11	8	10	
D	80	19	21	18	23	

Table 3.1: The learner's results table.

Focus

1   Complete the table by calculating the mean distances diffused by the red dye in each dish.
Write your answers in the table.

> **TIP**
>
> The learner measured the distances to the nearest whole millimetre. You therefore
> need to give the mean distances to the nearest whole millimetre as well.

2   Deduce whether the results support the learner's hypothesis or not.

Explain your answer.

....

....

....

Practice

3 State *four* variables that the learner kept constant, or that she should have kept constant, in the experiment.

First variable ....

Second variable ....

Third variable ....

Fourth variable ....

4 Explain why it was a good idea to have four holes in each dish, rather than only one.

....

....

5 Use your knowledge of diffusion to explain the pattern shown by the mean distances the red dye diffused at different temperatures.

....

....

....

....

Challenge

Sources of error are features of an experiment that reduce your trust in the results. Sources of error do not include mistakes that the learner might make, such as measuring a distance incorrectly. They are inbuilt uncertainties because of limitations of the apparatus, or the procedure.

An important source of error in the learner's experiment is the difficulty in deciding exactly where to measure to, because there is not a sharp edge where the colour of dye stops.

6 a Identify *one* other possible source of error in the learner's experiment, that would reduce the level of trust that she has in her results.

....

....

b Suggest how the learner could modify the experiment to reduce this source of error.

....

....

> Osmosis

KEY WORDS

high water potential: an area where there are a lot of water molecules – a dilute solution

low water potential: an area where there are not many water molecules
– a concentrated solution

osmosis: the diffusion of water molecules through a partially permeable membrane

osmosis (in terms of water potential): the net movement of water molecules from a region of higher water potential (dilute solution) to a region of lower water potential (concentrated solution) through a partially permeable membrane

partially permeable membrane: a membrane (very thin layer) that lets some particles move through it, but prevents others passing through

water potential gradient: a difference in water potential between two areas

Exercise 3.2

IN THIS EXERCISE YOU WILL:

- organise results and put them into a results chart
- identify anomalous results
- practise drawing a line graph
- suggest how an experiment can be improved.

A learner investigated the effect of different concentrations of sugar solutions on some potato cylinders.

He took a large potato and used a cork borer to cut out several cylinders, each exactly the same diameter. He removed the peel from the ends of the cylinders, and then cut them into exactly 1 cm lengths. He then measured the mass of each piece.

He placed one piece of potato in each of six beakers. He covered each piece with either water, or one of five different concentrations of sugar solution. He used the same volume of solution in each beaker.

The learner left the potato pieces in the beakers for 30 minutes. Then he removed them from the beakers, blotted them dry with filter paper and measured their mass again.

These were the results he wrote down.

Before   piece A = 5.2 g   piece B = 5.1 g   piece C = 4.9 g

                  piece D = 5.0 g   piece E = 5.1 g   piece F = 5.2 g

Solutions   A, distilled water   B, 0.1% sugar solution   C, 0.2% solution

                  D, 0.5% solution   E, 0.8% solution   F, 1.0% solution

After   A = 5.5 g   B = 5.2 g   C = 4.9 g

                  D = 5.3 g   E = 5.0 g   F = 5.0 g

Focus

7 Complete the results table. The first row has been done for you.

	Percentage concentration of solution	Mass / g		
		Before soaking	After soaking	Change
A	0.0	5.2	5.5	+0.3
B				
C				
D				
E				
F				

8 Deduce if there are any anomalous results. If you think there are, draw a ring around them.

9 Draw a line graph of the results, using the axes provided on the next page.

> **TIP**
>
> Plot each point as a small, neat cross, ×. Then use a ruler and a sharp pencil to draw straight lines between the points.
>
> Remember to ignore any anomalous results when you draw the lines on your graph.

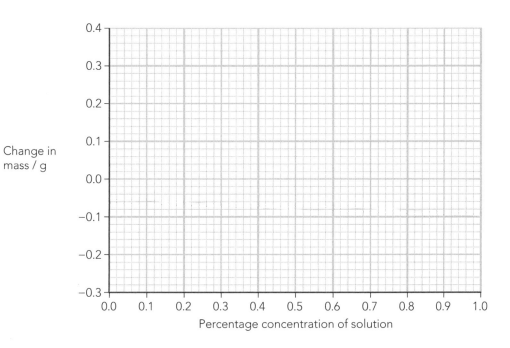

Change in mass / g (y-axis)

Percentage concentration of solution (x-axis)

Practice

10 Use your knowledge of osmosis to explain the results of this experiment.

....

....

....

....

....

....

....

11 Suggest how the learner could change his method to improve the trust he has in his results.

....

....

....

Challenge

12 The learner's teacher suggested that it would be better if he calculated the percentage change in mass of each piece of potato, rather than just the change in mass.

Do you agree? Explain your answer.

....

....

....

....

13 Suggest how the learner could use his results to estimate the concentration of the solution inside the cells in the potato.

....

....

....

....

....

....

› Active transport

> **KEY WORDS**
>
> **active transport:** the movement of molecules or ions through a cell membrane from a region of lower concentration to a region of higher concentration (i.e. against a concentration gradient) using energy from respiration
>
> **carrier proteins** (or **protein carriers**): protein molecules in cell membranes that can use energy to change shape and move ions or molecules into or out of a cell

Exercise 3.3

IN THIS EXERCISE YOU WILL:

- interpret data about ion concentrations
- make a prediction, based on data and your biological knowledge.

Focus

14 Draw lines to match each term with its description.

Term	Description
diffusion	movement of particles through a cell membrane, against a concentration gradient
concentration gradient	a difference in concentration between two places
osmosis	the diffusion of water through a partially permeable membrane
active transport	the net movement of particles down a concentration gradient

Practice

Table 3.2 shows the concentrations of three different ions inside the cells in a plant root and in the water in the soil.

Ion	Concentration in plant root cells / mol per dm³	Concentration in soil water / mol per dm³
A	0.5	0.5
B	1.0	0.4
C	0.6	0.8

Table 3.2: Concentrations of three different ions.

15 a Identify which ion has the same concentration in the root hair as in the soil water.

....

b Which process is most likely to explain how this ion moves between the root hair and soil water? Circle your answer.

active transport   diffusion   osmosis

16 Identify which ion has been moved *into* the root hair by active transport. ....

Explain your answer.

....

....

Challenge

17 If the soil in which the plant is growing is flooded with water, the roots can no longer get enough oxygen.

Suggest how this would affect the concentrations of ions **A**, **B** and **C** in the root cells.

Explain each of your suggestions.

....

....

....

....

....

....

....

....

> Chapter 4

Biological molecules

> Carbohydrates, fats and proteins

KEY WORDS

antibodies: proteins secreted by white blood cells, which bind to pathogens and help to destroy them

Benedict's solution: a blue liquid that turns orange-red when heated with reducing sugar

biuret reagent: a blue solution that turns purple when mixed with amino acids or proteins

carbohydrates: substances that include sugars, starch and cellulose; they contain carbon, hydrogen and oxygen

cellulose: a carbohydrate that makes up plant cell walls

DCPIP: a purple liquid that becomes colourless when mixed with vitamin C

emulsion: a liquid containing two substances that do not fully mix; one of them forms tiny droplets dispersed throughout the other

fats: lipids that are solid at room temperature

glucose: a sugar that is used in respiration to release energy

glycogen: a carbohydrate that is used as an energy store in animal cells

iodine solution: a solution of iodine in potassium iodide; it is orange-brown, and turns blue-black when mixed with starch

lipids: substances containing carbon, hydrogen and oxygen; they are insoluble in water and are used as energy stores in organisms

oils: lipids that are liquid at room temperature

pathogen: a microorganism that causes disease, such as bacteria

protein: a substance whose molecules are made of many amino acids linked together; each different protein has a different sequence of amino acids

reducing sugars: sugars such as glucose, which turn Benedict's solution orange-red when heated together

starch: a carbohydrate that is used as an energy store in plant cells

sugars: carbohydrates that have relatively small molecules; they are soluble in water and they taste sweet

---

Exercise 4.1: Focus

A learner carried out tests on two foods. This is what she wrote in her notebook.

Starch test – food A went brown, food B went black

Benedict's solution – food A went orange-red, food B went blue

1 Draw a results table in the space below and complete it to show the learner's results and conclusions. Think carefully about the best way of showing what she did, what she was testing for, what results she obtained and what these results mean.

> **TIP**
>
> Remember to state the actual colours that the student saw. Do not just write 'no change'. A good phrase to use is 'The solution changed colour from ....
> to ....'.

SELF-ASSESSMENT

How confident do you feel about drawing and completing a results table? Give yourself a mark for each of the points in the checklist. Award yourself:

2 marks   if you did it well

1 mark   if you made a good attempt at it and partly succeeded

0 marks   if you did not try to do it, or did not succeed

Checklist	Marks awarded
I used a ruler and sharp pencil to construct the table.	
I had a row (or column) headed 'Food'.	
I had a row (or column) headed 'Starch test' or 'Iodine test'.	
I had a row (or column) headed 'Reducing sugar test' or 'Benedict's test'.	
I included the starting colour, and the colour it changed to, for each test.	
I included a conclusion for each test, showing whether the starch or reducing sugar was present in the food.	
Total (out of 12):	

2   Complete this table about carbohydrates.

Example of carbohydrate	Function in organisms
glucose	
	the form in which plants store energy
cellulose	
glycogen	

Exercise 4.2: Practice

IN THIS EXERCISE YOU WILL:

- check that you remember how to test for proteins
- recall information about the functions of different parts of cells
- research a protein of your choice.

3   Describe how you would carry out the biuret test, to find out if a substance contains protein.

....

....

....

....

4   **a**   Name the part of a cell where proteins are synthesised (made).

....

b   Name the smaller molecules from which proteins are synthesised.

....

c   Explain why the sequence in which these smaller molecules are linked together is important.

....

....

....

5   There are thousands of different proteins in an organism. Choose *one* protein, and use the internet to find out about the function it has.

You could choose a protein from this list, or a different one if you prefer.

antibodies   haemoglobin   insulin

....

....

....

....

....

....

Exercise 4.3: Challenge

6   The biuret test is used to test foods for proteins. The intensity of the colour obtained depends
     on the concentration of protein in the sample being tested.

     Plan an investigation to test this hypothesis:

Milk from cows contains a higher concentration of protein than milk from goats.

     Include information about:

     • the variables you will change, standardise and measure

     • the apparatus and procedure you will use

     • predictions of the results you will obtain, if the hypothesis is correct

     • an outline results table that you could use.

....

....

....

....

....

....

....

....

....

....

....

....

....

....

....

....
....
....
....
....
....
....
....

> DNA

KEY WORDS

amino acids: substances with molecules containing carbon, hydrogen, oxygen and nitrogen; there are 20 different amino acids found in organisms

base: one of the components of DNA; there are four bases, A, C, G and T, and their sequence determines the proteins that are made in a cell

complementary base pairing: the way in which the bases of the two strands of DNA pair up; A always pairs with T, and C with G

DNA: a substance that makes up genes and chromosomes, providing instructions for making proteins in a cell

nucleotides: molecules that are linked together into long chains, to make up a DNA molecule

Exercise 4.4

IN THIS EXERCISE YOU WILL:

- recall work that you did earlier, on cells
- check your knowledge and understanding of the structure of DNA.

Focus

7   Complete the sentences about DNA, using words from the list. You can use each word once, more than once or not at all.

animal   bacterial   chromosomes   circle   cytoplasm

membrane   nucleus   plasmids

In an animal or plant cell, DNA is found in the .... It forms long

thread-like structures called ....

In .... cells, there is no nucleus. Instead, the DNA is free in the cytoplasm.

It is in the form of a .... These cells also contain smaller circles of DNA,

called ....

Practice

8   Figure 4.1 shows part of a DNA molecule.

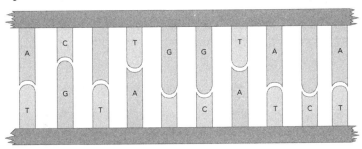

Figure 4.1: Part of a DNA molecule.

a   What are the parts labelled A, C, G and T? Circle the correct word.

amino acids   bases   genes   proteins

b   Complete the diagram by writing A, C, G or T in the three spaces.

Challenge

9   Complete these sentences.

A DNA molecule is made of two strands, coiled around each other to form a ....

....

Cross-links between the .... hold the two strands together.

The sequence of .... in a DNA molecule determines the sequence of

.... that are used to make protein molecules.

Chapter 5

Enzymes

> Biological catalysts

KEY WORDS

active site: the part of an enzyme molecule to which the substrate temporarily binds

complementary: with a perfect mirror-image shape

enzyme–substrate complex: the short-lived structure formed as the substrate binds temporarily to the active site of an enzyme

enzymes: proteins that are involved in all metabolic reactions, where they function as biological catalysts

product: the new substance formed by a chemical reaction

specificity: of enzymes, only able to act on a particular (specific) substrate

substrate: the substance that an enzyme acts upon

Exercise 5.1

IN THIS EXERCISE YOU WILL:

practise using the correct words to describe how enzymes work.

Focus

Figure 5.1 shows an enzyme and a molecule of its substrate.

This enzyme is able to split the substrate molecule into two product molecules.

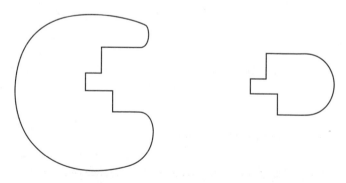

Figure 5.1: An enzyme and a molecule of its substrate.

---

1   On Figure 5.1 label these parts:

- the enzyme

- the active site of the enzyme

- the substrate.

Practice

2   In the space below, draw a diagram of the molecules that will be present after the enzyme in Figure 5.1 has changed the substrate into products.

Challenge

3   Use Figure 5.1 to explain why enzymes are specific to a particular substrate.

....

....

....

....

> Factors that affect enzymes

KEY WORDS

optimum: best; for example, the optimum temperature of an enzyme is the temperature at which its activity is greatest

range: the lowest to the highest value

Exercise 5.2: Focus

IN THIS EXERCISE YOU WILL:

practise thinking clearly about how enzymes work, and the factors that affect them.

4   Write a multiple-choice question for each of the following sets of answers. Write the correct answer to your question (A, B, C or D) on a separate piece of paper.

a   ....

....

....

A	amylase	B	catalase
C	lipase	D	protease

b   ....

....

....

A	denatured	B	killed
C	slowed down	D	speeded up

c   ....

....

....

A	active	B	catalyst
C	chemical	D	metabolic

5   Write *two* more multiple-choice questions about enzymes. For each question, give four answers to choose from – A, B, C or D. Write the correct answers to your questions on a separate piece of paper.

i   ....

....

....

....

....

....

ii ....

....

....

....

....

....

PEER ASSESSMENT

Exchange your questions with a partner.

Can you answer their questions correctly? Did they word their questions clearly?

Can they answer your questions correctly? Did you word your questions clearly, so that your partner understood and could choose the correct answer?

Exercise 5.3: Practice

IN THIS EXERCISE YOU WILL:

- use your knowledge and understanding to explain the results of an experiment
- suggest sources of error and improvements for an experiment.

A student carried out an experiment to investigate the effect of temperature on the enzyme lipase.

Lipase digests fats to fatty acids and glycerol. Fatty acids have a low pH.

The student made a solution of lipase and added equal volumes of it to five test-tubes.

The student treated the tubes as shown in Figure 5.2.

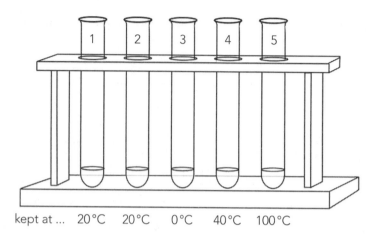

kept at ... 20°C   20°C   0°C   40°C   100°C

Figure 5.2: Solutions of lipase in test-tubes kept at different temperatures.

The student:

- kept all five tubes at these temperatures for five minutes
- used a pH meter to measure the pH of the liquid in each tube
- added equal volumes of milk (which contains fat) to tubes 2, 3, 4 and 5
- measured the pH of the contents of each tube, every two minutes.

The results are shown in Table 5.1.

Tube	1	2	3	4	5
Temp / °C	20				
Milk added?		yes			
pH at:					
0 mins	7.0	7.0	7.0	7.0	7.0
2 mins	7.0	6.8	7.0	6.7	7.0
4 mins	7.0	6.7	7.0	6.5	7.0
6 mins	7.0	6.6	7.0	6.3	7.0
8 mins	7.0	6.6	6.9	6.2	7.0
10 mins	7.0	6.5	6.9	6.2	7.0

Table 5.1: The student's results.

6 What is the substrate of the enzyme lipase?

....

7 What are the products when lipase acts on its substrate?

....

8 Explain why the pH becomes lower when lipase acts on its substrate.

....

....

9 Complete the table by filling in all the blank boxes.

> **TIP**
>
> The information to help you to do this is in the descriptions near the start of the question.

10 Explain why the pH did not change in tube 1.

....

11 Explain why the pH did not change in tube 5.

....

12 Explain why the results for tubes 2 and 3 differed from each other.

....

....

....

....

....

13 The student concluded that the optimum temperature for lipase is 40 °C. Evaluate the strength of the evidence for this conclusion. Explain your answer.

....

....

....

....

....

14 Suggest some changes that could be made to this experiment to obtain a more reliable or more precise value for the optimum temperature of lipase.

....

....

....

....

Exercise 5.4: Challenge

IN THIS EXERCISE YOU WILL:

practise planning an experiment.

15 The pH of a liquid can be kept steady by adding a buffer solution to it. You can obtain buffer solutions for any pH value you require. You can use a pH meter to measure the pH.

Plan an investigation to test this hypothesis:

> The optimum pH for amylase is 7.5.

Figure 5.3 shows some of the apparatus you might like to include.

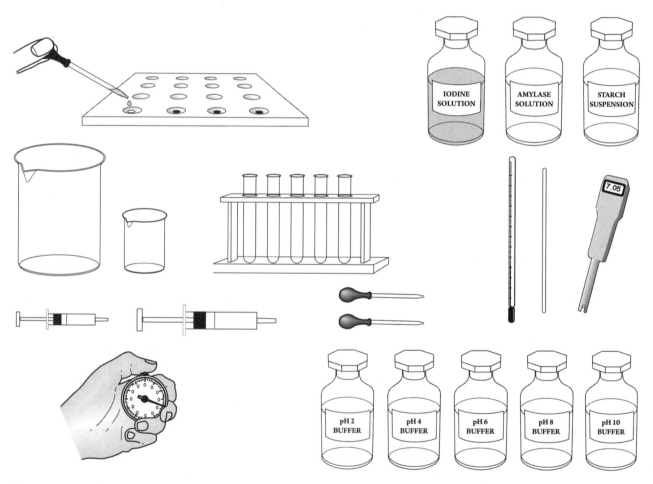

Figure 5.3: A selection of apparatus.

a What will you vary in your experiment?

....

b Over what range will you vary it?

....

c How will you vary it?

....

....

d What variables will you keep constant in your experiment? How will you do this?

....

....

....

e What results will you measure in your experiment? How will you measure them and when?

....

....

....

....

f Briefly outline the steps you will follow in your investigation.

....

....

....

....

....

....

....

....

....

....

g   In the space below, draw a results table in which you could record your results.

h   In the space below, sketch a graph to show the results you would expect if the hypothesis is correct. Remember to label the axes.

TIP

When you are asked to sketch a graph, draw two axes and label them. You do not need to add a scale to either axis. Then draw a line that is the shape you would expect to obtain.

SELF-ASSESSMENT

How confident do you feel about planning an experiment? Give yourself a mark for each of the points in the checklist. Award yourself:

2 marks if you did it well

1 mark if you made a good attempt at it and partly succeeded

0 marks if you did not try to do it, or did not succeed

Now ask your teacher to mark you.

Checklist	Marks awarded	
	You	Teacher
I can state the variable to be changed (independent variable), the range of this variable and how I will vary it.		
I can state at least three important variables to be kept constant (and not include ones that are not important).		
I can state the variable to be measured (dependent variable), how I will measure it and when I will measure it.		
I can draw a clear results table into which I can write my results.		
I can predict what the results will be if the hypothesis is correct.		
Total (out of 10):		

If you (or your teacher) gave yourself less than 10 marks, what can you do better if you do a similar task in future?

....

....

....

> Chapter 6

Plant nutrition

> Making carbohydrates using light energy; Leaves

KEY WORDS

chlorophyll: a green pigment (coloured substance) that absorbs energy from light; the energy is used to combine carbon dioxide with water and make glucose

cuticle: a thin layer of wax that covers the upper surface of a leaf

nectar: a sweet liquid secreted by many insect-pollinated flowers, to attract their pollinators

palisade mesophyll: the layer of cells immediately beneath the upper epidermis, where most photosynthesis happens

photosynthesis: the process by which plants synthesise carbohydrates from raw materials using energy from light

spongy mesophyll: the layer of cells immediately beneath the palisade mesophyll, where some photosynthesis happens; this tissue contains a lot of air spaces between the cells

stomata (singular: **stoma**): openings in the surface of a leaf, most commonly in the lower surface; they are surrounded by pairs of guard cells, which control whether the stomata are open or closed

sucrose: a sugar whose molecules are made of glucose and another similar molecule (fructose) linked together

Exercise 6.1

IN THIS EXERCISE YOU WILL:

* summarise the sources of the raw materials of photosynthesis, as well as its products

* look carefully at unfamiliar diagrams, make comparisons, and use what you can see to suggest answers to questions.

Focus

1   Write the word equation for photosynthesis.

....

If you are asked to write a word equation, do *not* use formulae or write a balanced equation.

2 Figure 6.1 shows a palisade cell. (It is a little unusual, as it has a strand of cytoplasm across the middle of the cell.)

Write short descriptions in each box, to explain how a palisade cell in a leaf gets what it needs for photosynthesis, and what happens to the products.

Use each of these words at least once.

air space   diffusion   epidermis   osmosis   phloem

root hair   starch   stoma   sucrose   transparent   xylem

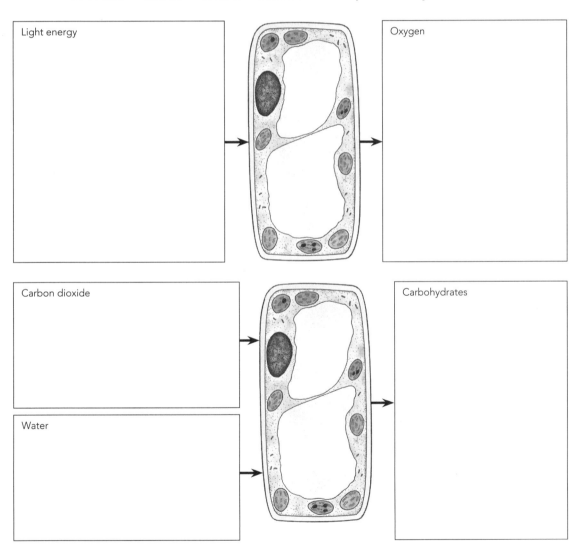

Light energy

Oxygen

Carbon dioxide

Water

Carbohydrates

Figure 6.1: A palisade cell.

Practice

Some of the leaves on a tree spend most of the day in bright sunlight, while others are in the shade. The diagrams in Figure 6.2 show sections through a leaf growing in the sunlight and a leaf growing in the shade.

a

b

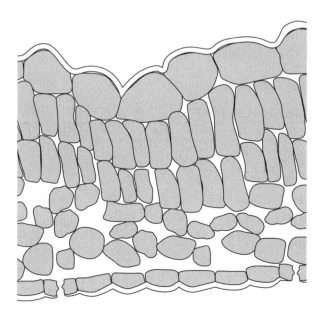

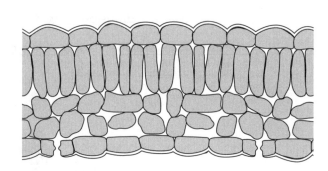

sun leaf

shade leaf

Figure 6.2: Sections of a leaf growing **a:** in the sunlight. **b:** in the shade.

3 On the *shade leaf* diagram (Figure 6.2b), label these tissues:

lower epidermis   **palisade mesophyll**   **spongy mesophyll**   **upper epidermis**

4 On the *shade leaf* diagram, draw a few green spots in each cell that you would expect to contain chloroplasts.

Challenge

5 Complete the table to compare the structures of each of these parts of the leaves shown in Figure 6.2.

> **TIP**
>
> When you make comparisons, try to use comparative words such as 'thicker'.

Part of leaf	Sun leaf	Shade leaf
cuticle		
palisade mesophyll		
spongy mesophyll		

6 Suggest an explanation for the difference in the cuticle that you have described in the table in **5**.

....

....

7 Suggest an explanation for the difference in the palisade layer that you have described in the table in **5**.

....

....

....

....

> **TIP**
>
> Do not panic when you see the command word 'suggest'! Think about what you know, then try to apply that to the situation you are being asked about.

> Factors affecting photosynthesis

Exercise 6.2

IN THIS EXERCISE YOU WILL:

- practise drawing a line graph
- use lines on a graph to interpret the factors affecting the rate of photosynthesis

> use your understanding of limiting factors to make a recommendation.

Focus

An experiment was performed to find out how fast a plant photosynthesised as the concentration of carbon dioxide in the air around it was varied. The results are shown in Table 6.1.

Percentage concentration of carbon dioxide	Rate of photosynthesis / arbitrary units
0.00	0
0.02	33
0.04	53
0.06	68
0.08	79
0.10	86
0.12	89
0.14	90
0.16	90
0.18	90
0.20	90

Table 6.1: A results table.

8 Plot these results on the grid below and draw a line.

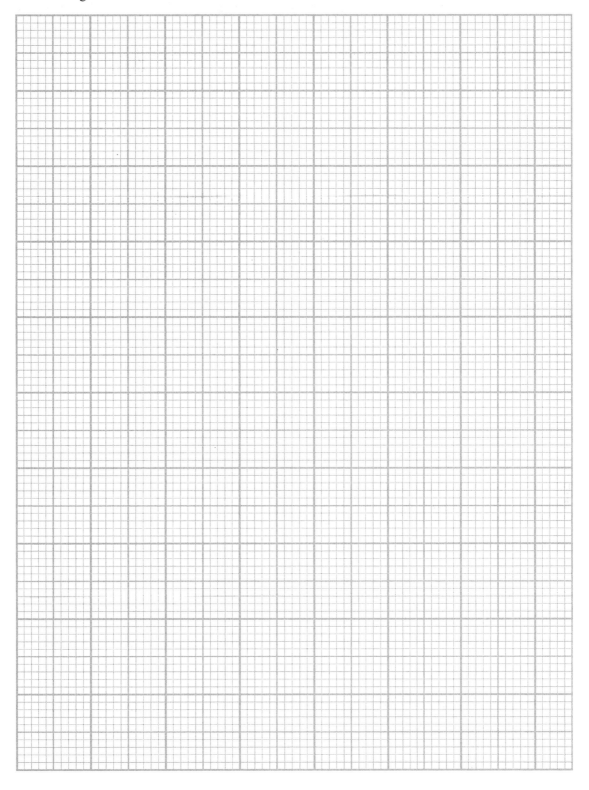

PEER ASSESSMENT

Exchange your graph with a partner. Give them a mark for each of the points in the checklist. When you swap back, write the marks you would give yourself in the last column. Are there any differences between the two marks? If so, why are the marks different?

For each point, award:

2 marks   if it was done really well

1 mark   if a good attempt was made

0 marks   if it was not attempted

Checklist	Marks awarded	
	Your partner	You
You have drawn the axes with a ruler, and used most of the width and height of the graph paper for the axis labels.		
You have used a good scale for the x-axis and the y-axis, going up in intervals of 10 on the y-axis, and 0.02 on the x-axis.		
You have included the correct unit with the scale that requires one.		
You have plotted each point precisely and correctly.		
You have used a small, neat cross for each point.		
You have drawn a single, clear line – either by ruling a line between each pair of points, or drawing a well-positioned best-fit line.		
Total (out of 12):		

9   Explain why the rate of photosynthesis increases as carbon dioxide concentration increases.

....

....

Practice

10 The experiment was repeated at a lower light intensity. The results are shown in Table 6.2.

Plot these values on your graph and draw a line. Label the two lines.

Percentage concentration of carbon dioxide	Rate of photosynthesis / arbitrary units
0.00	0
0.02	20
0.04	29
0.06	35
0.08	39
0.10	42
0.12	45
0.14	46
0.16	46
0.18	46
0.20	46

Table 6.2: Results at a lower light intensity.

11 State the carbon dioxide concentration of normal air.

....

12 Use your graph to determine the rate of photosynthesis in normal air in higher light intensity.

....

Challenge

13 Up to what concentration is carbon dioxide a limiting factor for photosynthesis in low light intensity?

....

14 Above this concentration (your answer to **13**), what is the limiting factor for photosynthesis when the plant is exposed to low light intensity?

....

15 Farmers and market gardeners often add carbon dioxide to the air in glasshouses where crops are growing. Use your graph to explain the advantage of doing this.

....

....

....

....

16 It is expensive to add carbon dioxide to glasshouses. Suggest a suitable concentration of carbon dioxide to add to a glasshouse in high light intensity, to obtain a good financial return from the sale of the crop. Explain your answer.

....

....

....

....

Chapter 7

Human nutrition

> Diet

Exercise 7.1

IN THIS EXERCISE YOU WILL:

practise finding and using relevant data in a table.

Table 7.1 shows the energy and nutrients contained in 100 g of five foods.

Food	Energy / kJ	Protein / g	Fat / g	Carbohydrate / g	Calcium / mg	Iron / mg	Vitamin C / mg	Vitamin D / mg
apple	150	0.2	0.0	9.0	0	0.2	2	0.0
chicken, roast	630	25.0	5.0	0.0	0	0.8	0	0.0
egg, scrambled	1050	10.0	23.0	0.0	60	2.0	0	1.8
rice, boiled	500	2.0	0.3	30.0	0	0.0	0	0.0
spinach, boiled	130	5.0	0.5	1.5	600	4.0	25	0.0

Table 7.1: The energy and nutrients contained in 100 g of five foods.

Focus

1   Which food contains the most energy per 100 g?

    ....

2   Which nutrients in the table provide energy?

    ....

3   Which nutrients in the table are mineral ions?

    ....

4   How many times more protein does roast chicken contain, than boiled rice?

....

Practice

5   What pattern can you see in the foods (in Table 7.1) that contain carbohydrate?

....

....

6   Scrambled egg has the highest energy content per gram of all of the foods in the table. What data in Table 7.1 could explain why the energy content of scrambled egg is so high?

....

....

7   A girl has anaemia. Which foods from the table would be most helpful for her to include in her diet? Explain your answer.

....

....

....

Challenge

8   Use the data in Table 7.1 to determine which of the five foods contains the greatest mass of water per 100 g. Show your working.

....

> Digestion and absorption

KEY WORDS

absorption: the movement of nutrients from the alimentary canal into the blood

bile: an alkaline fluid produced by the liver, which helps with fat digestion

bile duct: the tube that carries bile from the gall bladder to the duodenum

digestion: the breakdown of food

duodenum: the first part of the small intestine, into which the pancreatic duct and bile duct empty fluids

enamel: the very strong material that covers the surface of a tooth

gall bladder: a small organ that stores bile, before the bile is released into the duodenum

maltase: an enzyme that catalyses the breakdown of maltose to glucose

maltose: a reducing sugar made of two glucose molecules joined together

pancreas: a creamy-white organ lying close to the stomach, which secretes pancreatic juice; it also secretes the hormones insulin and glucagon, which are involved in the control of blood glucose concentration

salivary glands: groups of cells close to the mouth, which secrete saliva into the salivary ducts

small intestine: a long, narrow part of the alimentary canal, consisting of the duodenum and ileum

stomach: a wide part of the alimentary canal, in which food can be stored for a while, and where the digestion of protein begins

villi (singular: **villus**): very small finger-like projections that line the inner surface of the small intestine, greatly increasing its surface area

Exercise 7.2: Focus

IN THIS EXERCISE YOU WILL:

check that you understand the meanings of some terms relating to digestion and absorption.

9 Draw lines to match each term with its description.

Term	Description
pancreas	the breakdown of food into small molecules so that they can move from the intestine into the blood
absorption	an organ that secretes a juice containing hydrochloric acid
enamel	an enzyme that digests starch to reducing sugar
duodenum	the movement of nutrient molecules and ions through the wall of the intestine into the blood
amylase	the part of the alimentary canal into which bile and pancreatic juice flow
lipase	the outer, very hard layer of a tooth
stomach	an enzyme that breaks down its substrate to fatty acids and glycerol
digestion	an organ that produces enzymes that digest starch, protein and fat

Exercise 7.3: Practice

IN THIS EXERCISE YOU WILL:

add annotations to the correct part of a diagram of the digestive system.

Figure 7.1 shows the human digestive system.

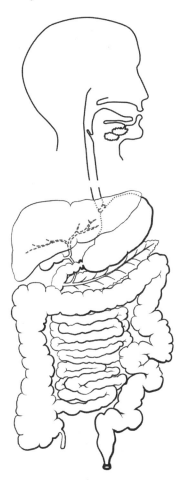

Figure 7.1: The human digestive system.

10 Add each label to the appropriate part of the diagram. Some of the labels should be written in two places.

Labels to add

- physical digestion increases the surface area of food (two places)

- the gall bladder

- amylase is secreted (two places)

- amylase acts on starch (two places)

- lipase breaks down fats

- absorption happens

- secretes a liquid with a low pH, which kills bacteria

- protease is secreted (two places)

SELF-ASSESSMENT

How confident do you feel about labelling a diagram of the digestive system?
Give yourself a rating for each of the points in the checklist, using:

☺ if you did it really well

😐 if you made a good attempt at it and partly succeeded

☹ if you did not try to do it, or did not succeed

Checklist	Rating
I drew the label lines with a ruler.	
Each label line touched the structure I meant to label.	
The label lines did not cross.	
The labels were written alongside the diagram, not on top of it.	
I got all twelve of the labels correct.	

Exercise 7.4: Challenge

IN THIS EXERCISE YOU WILL:

- practise describing what is shown in a graph

- apply your understanding of diet, digestion and absorption to a new context.

In an investigation into the absorption of vitamin D from the alimentary canal, a volunteer ate a measured quantity of vitamin D on a piece of toast. Blood samples were then taken from him at intervals over a period of 72 hours, and the concentration of vitamin D in each blood sample was measured.

The results are shown in the graph in Figure 7.2.

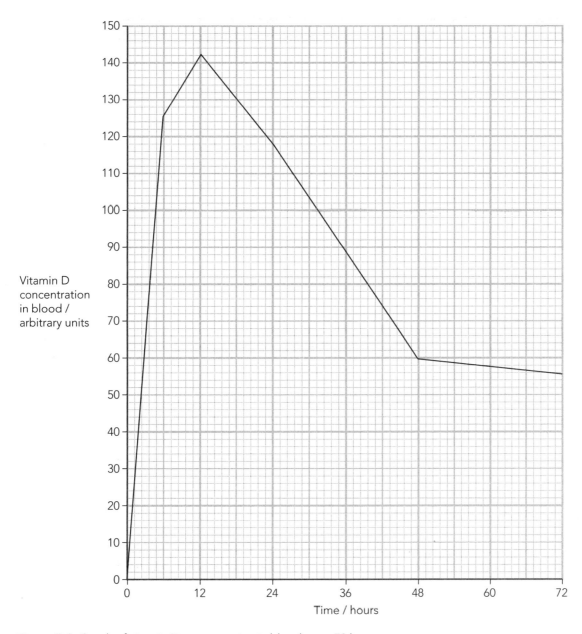

Figure 7.2: Graph of vitamin D concentration in blood, over 72 hours.

11 Describe the changes in the concentration of vitamin D in the blood over the 72-hour period (using the Tip box on the next page to help you).

....

....

....

....

....

> **TIP**
>
> When you describe a line graph, try to include:
>
> - what happens to the value on the *y*-axis, when the *x*-axis value increases (that is, state a general trend)
>
> - where the maximum or minimum values of the line occur, giving both the *x*-axis and *y*-axis values and their units
>
> - anywhere that the direction or gradient of the line changes, quoting the *x*-axis and *y*-axis values where this happens, including their units
>
> - a calculation – for example, the difference between the concentrations at two points on the graph.

12 Calculate the percentage change in vitamin D concentration between 12 hours and 48 hours.

Show your working. Give your answer to the nearest whole number.

> **TIP**
>
> $$\text{percentage change} = \frac{\text{change in value}}{\text{original value}} \times 100$$

....

13 Name the part of the alimentary canal in which vitamin D is absorbed into the blood.

....

14 Explain how this part of the alimentary canal is adapted to make absorption efficient.

....

....

....

....

....

15 Explain why vitamin D does not need to be digested before it is absorbed.

....

....

16 Vitamin D is soluble in fat, but insoluble in water. It is present in the fat component of foods that we eat.

   a Use this information to suggest how bile helps us to absorb vitamin D from food.

....

....

....

   b Suggest into which part of the villi it is absorbed. Explain your suggestion.

....

....

17 The volunteer was asked not to expose his skin to sunlight during the investigation. Suggest why this was done.

....

....

....

Chapter 8

Transport in plants

> Xylem and phloem

> **KEY WORDS**
>
> **lignin:** a hard, strong, waterproof substance that forms the walls of xylem vessels
>
> **phloem:** a plant tissue made up of living cells joined end to end; it transports substances made by the plant, such as sucrose and amino acids
>
> **xylem:** a plant tissue made up of dead, empty cells joined end to end; it transports water and mineral ions and helps to support the plant

Exercise 8.1

> **IN THIS EXERCISE YOU WILL:**
>
> - check that you know the functions of xylem and phloem
> - practise identifying tissues and calculating magnification
> - link the structure of xylem to its functions.

Focus

1 Complete the sentences, using words from the list.

> amino acids   fatty acids   leaves   mineral ions
>
> organ   roots   sucrose   tissue   water

Xylem is a .... that transports .... and ....

.... from the .... of a plant to its ....

Phloem transports .... and .... from the

leaves to other parts of the plant.

Practice

2 Figure 8.1 shows part of a buttercup root, seen using the high power lens of a light microscope.

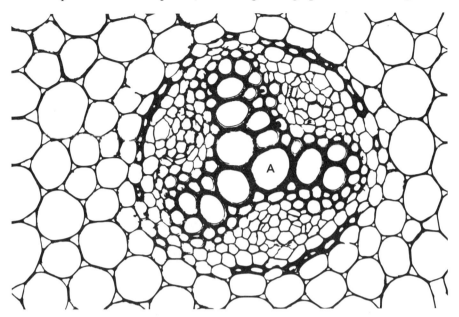

Figure 8.1: Photomicrograph of part of a buttercup root.

Use ruled lines to label these tissues:

cortex   phloem   xylem

3 The magnification of the image in Figure 8.1 is ×200.

Calculate the actual diameter of the cell labelled **A**.

Show your working. Give your answer in millimetres.

Diameter = ...

Challenge

4 Describe how the cells in xylem tissue are adapted for their functions.

....

....

....

....

....

> Transport of water

KEY WORD

transpiration: the loss of water vapour from leaves

Exercise 8.2

IN THIS EXERCISE YOU WILL:

- practise recording results
- draw a line graph, using best-fit lines
- analyse and evaluate results.

A student investigated this hypothesis:

Transpiration happens more quickly in windy conditions than in still air.

Figure 8.2 shows the apparatus that he used.

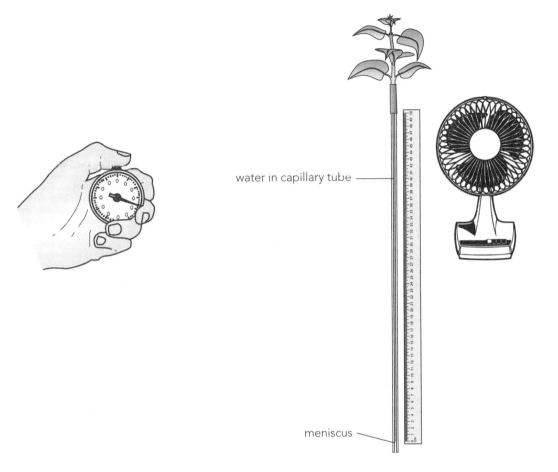

water in capillary tube

meniscus

Figure 8.2: Apparatus used in a transpiration investigation.

The student placed a leafy shoot in the apparatus and stood it in a place in the laboratory, where the air was still. He recorded the position of the meniscus every two minutes for ten minutes.

He then placed the fan close to the apparatus and switched it on. He continued to record the position of the meniscus every two minutes for the next ten minutes.

These are the results he wrote down.

start, 0 cm	2 mins, 2.8	4 mins, 6.1	6 mins, 10.0
8 mins, 12.9	10 mins, 16.2	12 mins, 21.8	14 mins, 27.9
16 mins, 31.1	18 mins, 39.5	20 mins, 44.9	

Focus

5   Draw a suitable results table in the space below, and complete it to show the student's results.

> **TIP**
>
> Remember to include the units in the table headings, and not in the table cells.

Practice

6   Plot these results on the grid on the next page.

- First, decide what to put on each axis. Then label the axes, including the units.

- Next, decide on a good scale for each axis. Make sure that you use at least half of the grid in each direction, and that your scale goes up in equal intervals.

- Plot the points as neat crosses, ×.

- Draw a vertical line upwards from the x-axis, to divide the graph into the period of time when the air was still, and when it was moving.

- Draw two best-fit lines, one on either side of this dividing line. If you think any of the results are anomalous, then ignore them when drawing your best-fit lines.

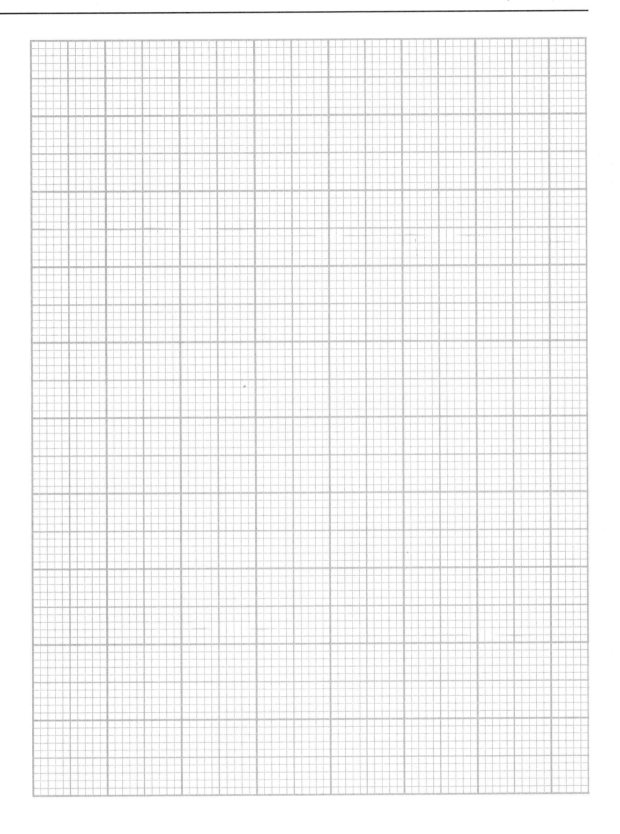

PEER ASSESSMENT

Exchange your graph with a partner. Rate their graph for each of the points in the checklist using:

☺ if they did it really well

😐 if they made a good attempt at it and partly succeeded

☹ if they did not try to do it, or did not succeed

Checklist	Rating
The axes are the right way round.	
The axes are fully labelled, with units.	
The scales on both axes are well chosen.	
The points are very neat with accurately placed crosses.	
The lines are best-fit lines, and are very clearly drawn.	

Challenge

7 Use your graph to calculate the mean rate of movement, in cm per minute, of the meniscus in:

    a still air; give your answer to three significant figures

                                                     ....

    b moving air; give your answer to three significant figures.

                                                     ....

8 Do the results support the student's hypothesis? Explain your answer.

....

....

....

....

9 Evaluate the student's method. For example, did the student control all the important variables? Did his method really measure what he thought he was measuring?

....

....

....

....

....

....

⟩ Translocation of sucrose and amino acids

KEY WORDS

sink: part of a plant to which sucrose or amino acids are being transported, and where they are used or stored

source: part of a plant that releases sucrose or amino acids, to be transported to other parts

Exercise 8.3

IN THIS EXERCISE YOU WILL:

- apply your understanding of sources and sinks to a new situation

- practise describing numerical results in words

- suggest explanations for results.

An experiment was carried out in Switzerland to investigate the movement of carbohydrates from sources to sinks in pine trees, *Pinus cembra*. Switzerland is a mountainous country in Europe.

Pine trees are coniferous trees, which keep their leaves all through the winter.

Focus

10   In which form are carbohydrates transported in phloem? Draw a circle around the correct answer.

glucose   starch   sucrose

11   In which form are carbohydrates stored in plant cells? Draw a circle around the correct answer.

glucose   starch   sucrose

12   In spring and summer in Switzerland, the leaves of pine trees photosynthesise.

Suggest *two* reasons why pine trees photosynthesise in spring and summer in Switzerland, but not in winter.

i   ....

ii   ....

Practice

13 Would you expect the leaves to be sources or sinks in spring and summer? Explain your answer.

....

....

....

14 Would you expect the leaves to be sources or sinks in winter? Explain your answer.

....

....

....

Table 8.1 shows the amount of starch, measured as a percentage of the dry mass of the tissues, in the leaves and roots of pine trees at three times of year.

Time of year	Starch in leaves / percentage of dry mass	Starch in roots / percentage of dry mass
spring	15.0	2.6
summer	15.6	3.1
autumn	4.9	4.1

Table 8.1: Amount of starch in leaves and roots in three seasons.

15 Describe the changes in the amount of starch in the pine tree *leaves* from spring until autumn.

TIP
Remember not to include reasons when you are asked to 'describe'.

....

....

....

16 Describe the changes in the amount of starch in the pine tree *roots* from spring until autumn.

....

....

....

17 Suggest reasons for the changes described in your answers to **15** and **16**.

....

....

....

....

....

Challenge

18 In summer, the researchers removed the buds from some pine trees, and the leaves from other pine trees. They left some pine trees untreated, to act as controls.

They measured the amount of starch in the leaves and buds of each group of trees at the end of the summer.

Their results are shown in Table 8.2.

Treatment	Starch in leaves / percentage of dry mass	Starch in buds / percentage of dry mass
control	4.9	7.1
buds removed	4.9	
leaves removed		6.5

Table 8.2: Amount of starch in leaves and buds in three groups of trees.

Describe *and* explain the results shown in the table.

....

....

....

....

....

....

....

....

....

....

> Chapter 9
Transport in animals

> Circulatory systems

KEY WORDS
circulatory system: a system of blood vessels with a pump and valves to ensure one-way flow of blood
deoxygenated blood: blood containing only a little oxygen
double circulatory system: a system in which blood passes through the heart twice on one complete circuit of the body
oxygenated blood: blood containing a lot of oxygen
single circulatory system: a system in which blood passes through the heart only once on one complete circuit of the body
valves: structures that allow a liquid to flow in one direction only

Exercise 9.1

IN THIS EXERCISE YOU WILL:
• check your understanding of the basic structure of the human circulatory system
> explain the advantages of a double circulation.

Focus

1   Complete the following sentences about the human circulatory system.

The circulatory system is a system of .... in which

blood is transported. The heart acts as a .... to move the blood. There are

.... in the circulatory system, which ensure a one-way flow of blood.

2   Figure 9.1 shows a simple plan of the human circulatory system.

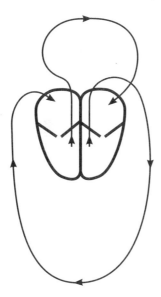

Figure 9.1: A simple plan of the human circulatory system.

On Figure 9.1:

• shade in red the parts of the heart that contain oxygenated blood

• shade in blue the parts that contain deoxygenated blood.

Practice

3   In the space next to Figure 9.1, draw a similar diagram to show a single circulatory system.

4   Name *one* organism that has a single circulatory system.

    ....

Challenge

5   Many animals with double circulatory systems have higher metabolic rates than those with single circulatory systems. Suggest an explanation for this.

    ....

    ....

    ....

    ....

    ....

    ....

> The heart

KEY WORDS

aorta: the largest artery in the body, which receives oxygenated blood from the left ventricle and delivers it to the body organs

atria: the thin-walled chambers at the top of the heart, which receive blood

pulmonary artery: the artery that carries deoxygenated blood from the right ventricle to the lungs

pulmonary veins: the veins that carry oxygenated blood from the lungs to the left atrium of the heart

vena cava: the large vein that brings deoxygenated blood to the right atrium

ventricles: the thick-walled chambers at the base of the heart, which pump out blood

Exercise 9.2: Focus

IN THIS EXERCISE YOU WILL:

practise naming the parts of the heart and describing their functions.

Figure 9.2 shows a section through a human heart.

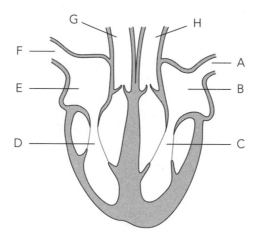

Figure 9.2: A section through a human heart.

6   Write the letter of each structure in the table. The first one has been done for you.

Then complete the table by writing the function of each structure.

Structure	Letter	Function
aorta	H	transports oxygenated blood to body cells
right ventricle		
left atrium		
left ventricle		
right atrium		
pulmonary artery		
pulmonary vein		
vena cava		

Exercise 9.3: Practice

IN THIS EXERCISE YOU WILL:

practise finding and using relevant figures in a complex set of data.

Table 9.1 shows part of a chart that doctors have used to predict the likelihood of a woman having a heart attack. Diabetes is an illness caused by a faulty mechanism for regulating the concentration of glucose in the blood. It can be controlled, but not cured.

	Percentage of women who are expected to have a heart attack within five years							
	Age 40		Age 50		Age 60		Age 70	
	No diabetes	With diabetes	No diabetes	With diabetes	No diabetes	With diabetes	No diabetes	With diabetes
Non-smokers	1	3	3	7	5	12	7	23
Smokers	4	7	6	13	12	22	15	33

Table 9.1: Data used to predict the likelihood of a heart attack in women.

7   Imagine that you are a doctor. A female patient is 54 years old. She has diabetes and she smokes.

What will you tell her about her chance of having a heart attack within the next five years?

....

....

....

8 What will you tell her she should do to reduce her chances of having a heart attack? How will you use the chart to explain this to her?

....

....

....

....

....

9 Suggest how the figures used in this chart have been determined.

....

....

....

....

Exercise 9.4: Challenge

IN THIS EXERCISE YOU WILL:

- practise reading new information carefully

- apply your knowledge of the human circulatory system in a new context.

Figure 9.3 shows the heart of a fetus (a baby that is still developing in its mother's uterus).

In a fetus, the lungs do not work. The fetus gets its oxygen from the mother, to whom it is connected by the umbilical cord. This cord contains a vein, which carries the oxygenated blood to the fetus's vena cava.

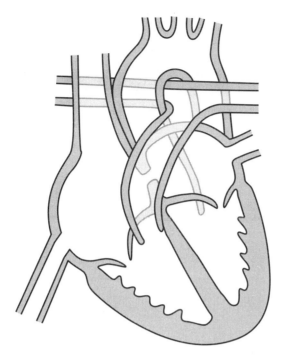

Figure 9.3: The heart of a fetus.

10 On Figure 9.3, write the letter **O** in the chamber of the heart that first receives oxygenated blood in an adult person.

11 On Figure 9.3, write the letters **OF** in the chamber of the heart that first receives oxygenated blood in a fetus.

12 If you look carefully at Figure 9.3, you can see that there is a hole in the septum between the left and right atria. Suggest the function of this hole in the heart of a fetus.

....

....

....

....

13 When the baby is born, it takes its first breath. The hole in the septum of the heart quickly closes.

Explain why this is important.

....

....

....

....

> Blood vessels and blood

KEY WORDS

haemoglobin: a red pigment found in red blood cells, which can combine reversibly with oxygen; it is a protein

pathogens: microorganisms that cause disease

plasma: the liquid part of blood

platelets: tiny cell fragments present in blood, which help with clotting

red blood cells: biconcave blood cells with no nucleus, which transport oxygen

white blood cells: blood cells with a nucleus, which help to defend against pathogens

Exercise 9.5: Focus

IN THIS EXERCISE YOU WILL:

- practise identifying features of blood vessels
- check that you remember the functions of the different components of blood.

14 Complete the table by placing a tick (✓) or cross (✗) in each space. One row has been done for you.

Feature	Arteries	Veins	Capillaries
contain valves			
wall is one cell thick			
carry blood at high pressure	✓	✗	✗
have a wide lumen			

15 Draw *one* line from each component (part) of blood to its function.

Component

Component
red blood cell

| plasma |

| white blood cell |

| platelet |

Function

| transport nutrients |

| destroy pathogens |

| clotting |

| transport oxygen |

Exercise 9.6: Practice

IN THIS EXERCISE YOU WILL:

practise organising an answer to a question that requires extended writing.

16 Arteries carry blood at high pressure, while veins carry blood at low pressure.

Explain how their structures are related to these functions.

TIP

Start by making a list of bullet points of all the relevant information you can think of. Then organise your points into a logical sequence. Write your final answer in full sentences.

....

....

....

....

....

....

....

....

....

PEER ASSESSMENT

Exchange your answer with a partner. Rate their answer for each of the points in the checklist using:

☺   if they did it really well

😐   if they made a good attempt at it and partly succeeded

☹   if they did not try to do it, or did not succeed

Checklist	Rating
The answer was written in full sentences.	
The answer was written in a sensible sequence, so that it was easy to follow.	
The answer referred to the thickness of the walls of arteries and veins.	
The answer correctly explained why arteries and veins have walls with different thicknesses.	
The answer referred to the quantity of elastic tissue in the walls of arteries and veins.	
The answer correctly explained why arteries and veins have walls with different amounts of elastic tissue.	
The answer referred to valves in veins, and explained why veins need valves and arteries do not.	

Exercise 9.7: Challenge

IN THIS EXERCISE YOU WILL:

- practise describing what is shown on a graph
- apply your knowledge of the transport of oxygen in a new situation.

The air is much thinner at high altitude, so less oxygen is drawn into the lungs with each breath. When a person who normally lives at low altitude travels into high mountains, changes occur in their blood system.

The bar chart in Figure 9.4 shows changes in the pulse rate and the number of red blood cells in a person who moved to high altitude, stayed there for two years, and then returned to sea level.

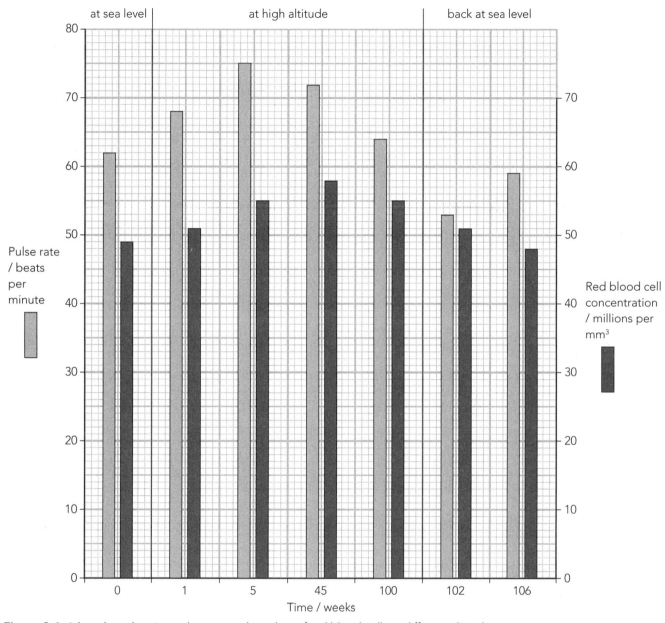

Figure 9.4: A bar chart showing pulse rate and number of red blood cells at different altitudes.

17 Describe the changes in the pulse rate over the period shown in Figure 9.4.

....

....

....

....

....

....

18 Describe the changes in the number of red blood cells over the period shown in Figure 9.4.

....

....

....

....

....

....

19 State the function of red blood cells.

....

20 Suggest a reason for the change in the number of red blood cells during the first year of
the study.

....

....

....

....

....

21 Muscles need a good supply of oxygen in order to be able to work hard and fast. Athletes
often train at high altitude for several months before a major competition that will be held at
a lower altitude.

Use the data in the graph to suggest how this might help them to perform well in
the competition.

....

....

....

....

....

....

Chapter 10

Diseases and immunity

> Transmission of pathogens

KEY WORDS
pathogen: a microorganism that causes disease, such as bacteria
transmissible disease: a disease that can be passed from one host to another; transmissible diseases are caused by pathogens

Exercise 10.1: Focus

IN THIS EXERCISE YOU WILL:
• check that you understand the meanings of some important words
• try to give clear descriptions of processes, in your own words.

Colds are caused by viruses. We can get a cold if we breathe in droplets of moisture breathed out by someone else who has a cold.

1   Which word in the sentences above refers to a pathogen?

    ....

2   Is a cold a transmissible disease? Explain your answer.

    ....

    ....

3   Outline how each of these body defences helps to protect us from pathogens.

   a   stomach acid

   ....

   ....

   b   white blood cells

   ....

   ....

   ....

   ....

   ....

Exercise 10.2: Practice

IN THIS EXERCISE YOU WILL:

•   practise constructing a bar chart

•   make suggestions to explain data provided.

Table 10.1 shows the number of reported cases of food poisoning caused by five different pathogens. It also shows the percentage of these reported cases caused by each pathogen.

Pathogen	Number of cases	Percentage of cases
Norovirus	5 461 731	58
Salmonella	1 027 561	11
Clostridium	965 958	10
Campylobacter	845 024	9
Staphylococcus	241 148	3

Table 10.1: Cases of food poisoning in the USA in 2011, caused by five pathogens.

4 Explain what is meant by the term *pathogen*.

....

....

5 Plot the data for the percentage of cases caused by each pathogen as a bar chart.

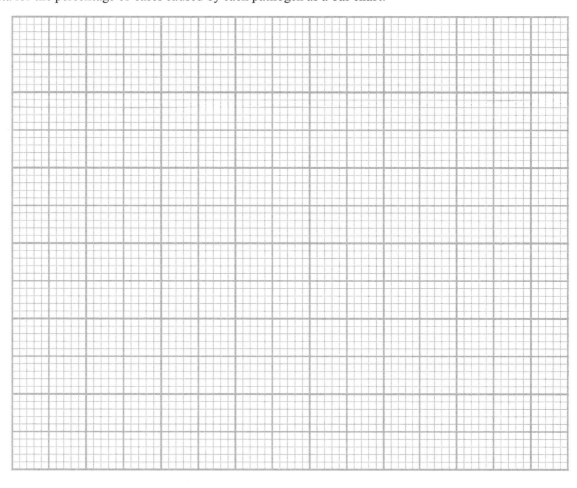

6 Suggest why the percentage of cases caused by these five pathogens does not add up to 100.

....

....

....

7 Suggest why the actual number of cases of food poisoning may have been much greater than the numbers shown in the table.

....

....

....

8   List *three* measures that people can take to avoid food poisoning in their home.

   i   ....

   ii   ....

   iii   ....

Exercise 10.3: Challenge

IN THIS EXERCISE YOU WILL:

- practise writing an answer where you are not given much help to structure it

- practise calculating a percentage increase.

The graph in Figure 10.1 shows information about the mass of solid waste generated in Australia in 2002–2003 and in 2006–2007, and how this waste was disposed of.

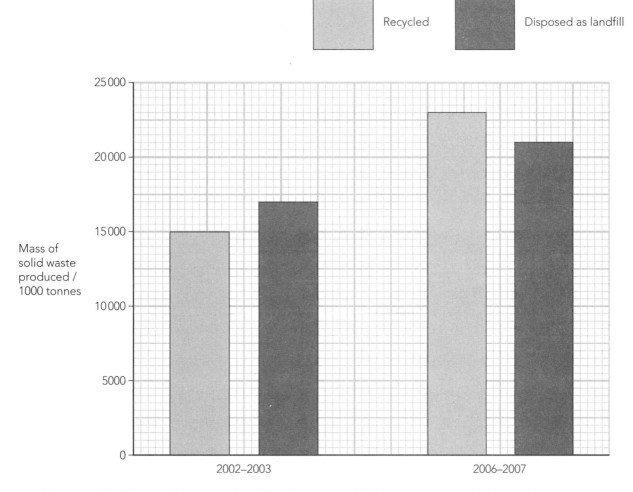

Figure 10.1: Mass of solid waste disposed as landfill and mass recycled for two time periods in Australia.

9 Compare the data for 2006–2007 with the data for 2002–2003. (You should be able to think of at least three different comparisons to make, but see if you can make four.) Use numbers from the graph to support your comparisons.

> TIP
>
> Start by thinking what you can compare and make a list. Then make notes for each comparison, remembering to try to use numbers where you can. Do not start writing your final answer until you have done this. Use comparative words in your answer – such as 'more' and 'bigger increase'.

....

....

....

....

....

....

....

10 Suggest the benefits of increasing the amount of waste that we recycle, rather than disposing of it in landfill sites.

....

....

....

....

....

....

....

11 a   Calculate the total mass of waste produced in 2002–2003 and in 2006–2007.
Show your working.

Total waste in 2002–2003 ....

Total waste in 2006–2007 ....

b   Calculate the increase in total waste between 2002–2003 and 2006–2007.

....

c   Use your answer to **b** to calculate the percentage increase in waste between 2002–2003 and
2006–2007, using this formula:

$$\text{percentage increase} = \frac{\text{increase in total waste}}{\text{total waste in 2002–2003}} \times 100$$

Show your working.

....

> # The immune response

Exercise 10.4

IN THIS EXERCISE YOU WILL:

- analyse data presented in a complex graph
- think about the difference between correlation and causation
- apply your knowledge of DNA in a new context.

Focus

Polio (short for poliomyelitis) is a disease caused by a virus, which is transmitted from one person to another through food or water contaminated with faeces from an infected person. Many people show no symptoms when they are infected, but in a small percentage of cases, the virus enters the spinal cord and causes damage to neurones that normally send nerve impulses to muscles. This results in paralysis. Polio is much more common in young children than in adults.

The World Health Organization (WHO) is committed to eradicating polio from the world. This is being done by a vaccination programme.

The graph in Figure 10.2 shows the estimated number of cases of polio in the world between 1980 and 2005, and the percentage of children who were vaccinated each year.

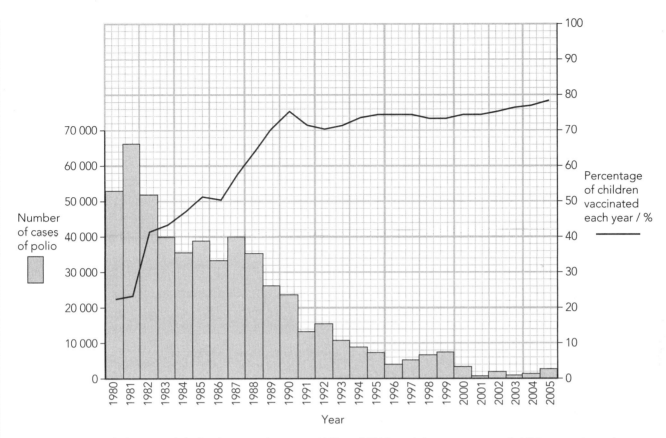

Figure 10.2: Graph showing global polio cases between 1980 and 2005, and the percentage of children vaccinated.

12 Suggest why children are more likely to get polio than adults. (You may be able to think of more than one reason.)

....

....

....

13 Describe the changes in the numbers of polio cases between 1980 and 2005.

TIP
Remember to quote figures from the graph in your answer.

....

....

....

....

....

Practice

14 Evaluate how well the data in the graph in Figure 10.2 support the conclusion that vaccination has caused a decrease in polio cases.

> **TIP**
>
> Remember that correlation does not always imply causation; however, we might still be able to assume causation if we can give a good explanation for it.

....

....

....

....

....

15 The polio vaccine is unusual, because it can be given by mouth rather than by injection.

Suggest why most vaccines have to be given by injection.

> **TIP**
>
> Think about what happens inside the alimentary canal.

....

....

....

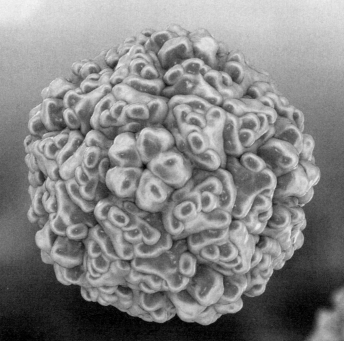

Challenge

16 The polio vaccine contains polio viruses that have been treated to make them unable to reproduce in the body.

Explain how the polio vaccine makes a person immune to polio.

....

....

....

....

....

....

....

17 Polio viruses contain DNA. The DNA codes for proteins that the virus can make when it is inside a host cell.

The viruses in the polio vaccine have DNA in which the base sequence has several differences from the base sequence in the normal polio virus.

Suggest how this makes the viruses in the vaccine unable to reproduce in the human body.

....

....

....

....

....

....

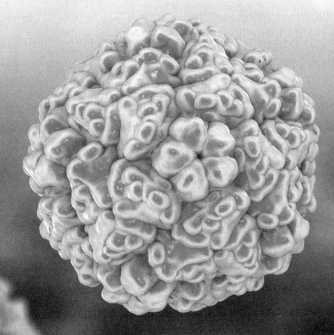

Respiration and gas exchange

> Respiration

Exercise 11.1: Focus

IN THIS EXERCISE YOU WILL:

check your understanding of respiration, by correcting someone else's mistakes.

1   Here are some statements that a student made, about respiration.

Each statement has a mistake in it.

Rewrite each statement, correcting the mistakes.

a   Every cell uses energy to help it to respire.

....

....

b   Aerobic respiration produces energy by combining nutrient molecules, such as glucose, with oxygen.

....

....

c   Anaerobic respiration happens in mitochondria.

....

....

d   In human muscle, both aerobic respiration and anaerobic respiration produce carbon dioxide.

....

....

e   Anaerobic respiration releases much more energy from each glucose molecule than aerobic respiration does.

....

....

Exercise 11.2: Practice

A student had a fish tank in which she kept tropical fish. She knew it was meant to be a good idea to keep living plants in the tank as well. She wanted to find out how the plants affected the concentration of carbon dioxide in the water.

Figure 11.1 shows the apparatus that she set up. She used hydrogencarbonate indicator solution because it is yellow when it contains a large amount of carbon dioxide, orange with a small amount and red when it contains no carbon dioxide at all.

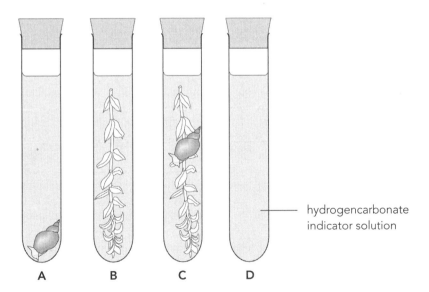

hydrogencarbonate
indicator solution

Figure 11.1: A student's apparatus.

The student left all four tubes in a sunny place for 30 minutes. When she looked at the tubes again, she found the indicator had turned yellow in tube A, deep red in tube B, and stayed orange in tubes C and D.

2 Draw a results table in the space below and fill it in to show the student's results.

3 Explain the results in each tube.

TIP
Remember that living organisms all respire all the time, and that plants also photosynthesise in the light.

Tube A

....

....

Tube B

....

....

Tube C

....

....

Tube D

....

....

4   Predict the results that would be obtained if all the tubes were left in the dark.

....

....

....

....

5   Discuss what these results and your predictions in **4** suggest about whether or not it is good to have living plants in a fish tank.

....

....

....

....

Exercise 11.3: Challenge

IN THIS EXERCISE YOU WILL:

plan an experiment, without any help with structuring your answer.

6   Plan an investigation to test this hypothesis:

> Germinating peas respire faster as temperature increases, up to an optimum.

Think carefully about controlling variables, what you will measure and when, and how you will keep yourself and others safe. Describe how you will record, display and interpret your results. Predict what the results will be if the hypothesis is correct.

....

....

....

....

....

....

....

....

....

....

SELF-ASSESSMENT

Assess your plan. Rate yourself for each of the points in the checklist, using these colours:

Green   if you did it well

Amber   if you made a good attempt at it and partly succeeded

Red   if you did not try to do it, or did not succeed

Checklist	Colour
I stated clearly what the independent variable is and described how I would change it.	
I suggested five different temperatures that I would use.	
I stated clearly what the dependent variable is and described how I would measure it.	
I identified at least two important variables that should be kept the same and described how I would do this.	
I made a list, or gave a description, of all the apparatus and materials I would use.	
I described how I would keep myself and others safe as I worked.	
I drew an outline results table with headings.	
I sketched a graph, with the axes labelled, to show what I predict the results would be if the hypothesis is correct.	

> Gas exchange

KEY WORDS

alveoli: tiny air-filled sacs in the lungs where gas exchange takes place

gas exchange: the diffusion of oxygen and carbon dioxide into and out of an organism's body

gas exchange surface: a part of the body where gas exchange between the body and the environment takes place

Exercise 11.4

IN THIS EXERCISE YOU WILL:

- practise handling data provided in a table, including making a calculation
- compare two sets of data
- use information provided, and your own understanding, to suggest an explanation for patterns in data.

Focus

Rat lungs have a similar structure to human lungs. Researchers measured the surface area of the alveoli in the lungs of female and male rats of different ages. They also measured the mass of each rat, and calculated the number of square centimetres of alveolar surface area per gram of body mass.

Their results are shown in Table 11.1.

Age / days	Ratio of alveolar surface area to body mass / cm² per gram	
	Females	Males
21	21.6	23.1
33	15.4	15.2
45	12.9	12.1
60	13.4	10.9
95	13.4	9.4

Table 11.1: Ratio of alveolar surface area to body mass in male and female rats.

7 Plot line graphs on the grid below to display these data. Plot both curves on the same pair of axes.

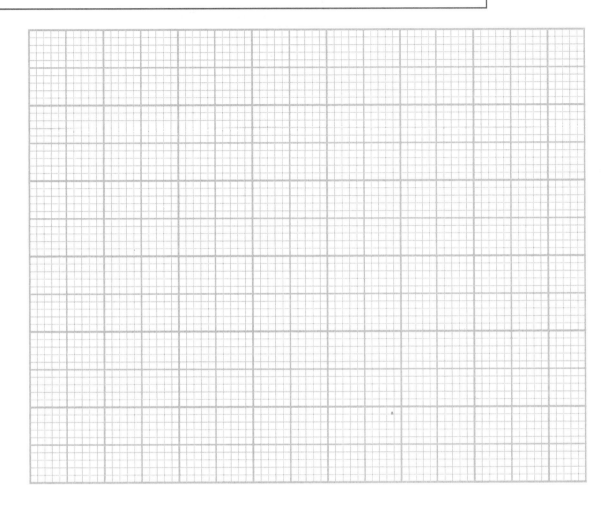

8   A 21-day-old male rat has a body mass of 40 g.

Using the data in Table 11.1, calculate this rat's probable alveolar surface area.

Show your working.

> **TIP**
>
> Look at the ratio of alveolar surface area to body mass for a 21-day-old male rat.
>
> This tells you how many cm² of surface there are for each gram of body mass.

....

Practice

9   Suggest why the researchers recorded the ratio of alveolar surface area to body mass, rather than just the alveolar surface area.

....

....

....

10 Compare the results for female and male rats, shown in Table 11.1.

....

....

....

....

....

....

Challenge

11 Female rats are able to become pregnant when they are about 60 days old. Their lungs then have to supply oxygen for themselves, and also for their developing offspring.

Suggest how the data in Table 11.1 could relate to this fact.

....

....

....

....

....

Chapter 12

Coordination and response

> The human nervous system

KEY WORDS

axon: a long, thin, fibre of cytoplasm that extends from the cell body of a neurone

central nervous system (CNS): the brain and spinal cord

motor neurone: a neurone that transmits electrical impulses from the central nervous system to an effector

nerve impulse: an electrical signal that passes rapidly along an axon

neurone: a cell that is specialised for conducting electrical impulses rapidly

peripheral nervous system (PNS): the nerves outside the brain and spinal cord

receptors: cells or groups of cells that detect stimuli

reflex action: a rapid, automatic response to a stimulus, that does not involve conscious thought

reflex arc: a series of neurones (sensory, relay and motor) that transmit electrical impulses from a receptor to an effector

relay neurone: a neurone that transmits electrical impulses within the central nervous system

sensory neurone: a neurone that transmits electrical impulses from a receptor to the central nervous system

stimuli: changes in the environment that can be detected by organisms

synapse: a junction between two neurones

Exercise 12.1: Focus

IN THIS EXERCISE YOU WILL:

practise using the new vocabulary for this topic.

1   Complete the sentences about the human nervous system, using words from the list.

axon   central   chemical   electrical   neurones

peripheral   receptors   stimulus

The human nervous system is made of specialised cells called .... These

cells have a long thread of cytoplasm called an .... They can transmit

.... impulses very quickly.

The brain and spinal cord make up the .... nervous system. The nerves outside

the brain and spinal cord form the .... nervous system.

Exercise 12.2: Practice

IN THIS EXERCISE YOU WILL:

check that you understand reflex arcs.

Figure 12.1 shows a reflex arc.

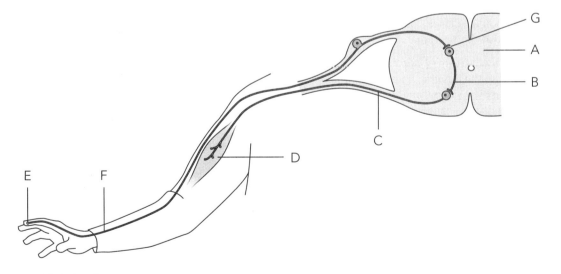

Figure 12.1: A reflex arc.

2 Complete the table below to identify the labelled structures in Figure 12.1.

Letter	Name
A	
B	
C	
D	
E	
F	
G	

3 On Figure 12.1, draw *one* arrow on each of parts B, C and F, to show the direction in which a nerve impulse travels.

Exercise 12.3: Challenge

IN THIS EXERCISE YOU WILL:

plan an experiment, with no help.

4 Reaction time is the time between receiving a stimulus and responding to it.

Here is a method for measuring reaction time.

- Ask your partner to hold a ruler vertically, with the 0 at the bottom.

- Place your hand at the bottom of the ruler, exactly opposite the 0 mark, ready to catch it. Rest your hand on the bench, so that it cannot change its position (see Figure 12.2).

- Your partner lets go of the ruler, and you catch it as quickly as you can.

- Read off the distance on the ruler where you have caught it. The faster your reaction time, the shorter the distance.

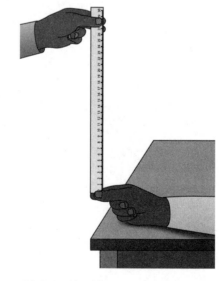

Figure 12.2: Method for measuring reaction time.

Plan an experiment to test this hypothesis:

Consuming drinks containing caffeine decreases reaction time.

....

....

....

....

....

....

....

....

....

....

....

....

....

....

....

....

....

....

....

....

....

> Sense organs

KEY WORDS

accommodation: changing the shape of the lens to focus on objects at different distances from the eye

antagonistic muscles: a pair of muscles whose contraction has opposite effects; when one contracts, the other relaxes

ciliary muscle: a circle of muscle surrounding the lens, and joined to it by the suspensory ligaments; when it contracts, it slackens the ligaments so that the lens becomes fatter

cornea: a transparent layer near the front of the eye, which refracts light rays entering the eye

iris: the coloured part of the eye; it contains muscles that can alter the size of the pupil

iris reflex (pupil reflex): an automatic response to a change in light intensity; the receptors are in the retina, and the effector is the muscles in the iris

lens: a transparent structure in the eye, which changes shape to focus light rays onto the retina

optic nerve: the nerve that carries electrical impulses from the retina to the brain

pupil: a circular gap in the middle of the iris, through which light can pass

retina: a tissue at the back of the eye that contains receptor cells that respond to light

suspensory ligaments: strong, inelastic fibres that hold the lens in position; when they are under tension, they pull the lens into a thinner shape

Exercise 12.4: Focus

IN THIS EXERCISE YOU WILL:

check that you know the names and functions of the parts of the eye.

Figure 12.3 shows a human eye.

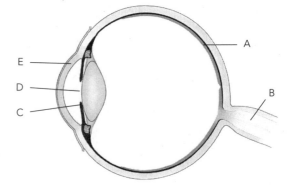

Figure 12.3: A human eye.

5   Complete the table, by naming each structure and stating its function.

Letter	Name	Function
A		
B		
C		
D		
E		

Exercise 12.5: Practice

IN THIS EXERCISE YOU WILL:

practise describing and explaining the iris (pupil) reflex.

6   When a person moves from a brightly lit place into darkness, the diameter of the pupil increases.

Complete the sentences that describe this change and how it is brought about.

As you move into darkness, the intensity of light falling onto the eye ....

This is sensed by cells in the .... of the eye. They send an electrical impulse along

the .... nerve to the brain.

The brain then sends an impulse to the muscles in the iris of the eye. The radial muscles

.... and the circular muscles ...., which makes the diameter of the

pupil increase.

This is an example of a .... action.

Exercise 12.6: Challenge

IN THIS EXERCISE YOU WILL:

explain how the eye focuses on objects at different distances.

Figure 12.4 shows an eye focused on a distant object.

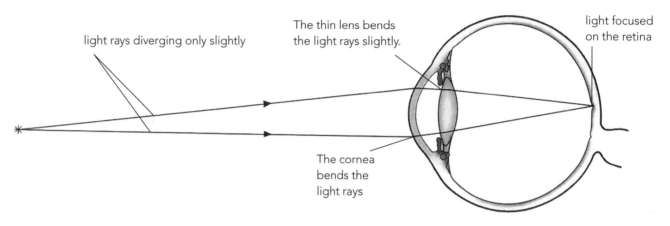

Figure 12.4: An eye focused on a distant object.

7 Complete Figure 12.5 to show the eye when it is focused on a nearby object. Add labels to match those on Figure 12.4.

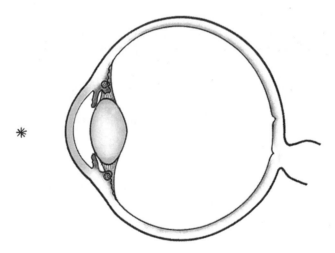

Figure 12.5: An eye focused on a nearby object.

8   Describe how the changes that you have shown are brought about. Use these words in your description:

ciliary muscles   lens   suspensory ligaments

....

....

....

....

....

....

9   As people get older, their lenses become less able to change shape. Suggest how this may affect their vision.

....

....

....

....

〉 Hormones

KEY WORDS

adrenaline: a hormone secreted by the adrenal glands, which prepares the body for fight or flight

endocrine glands: glands that secrete hormones

hormones: chemicals that are produced by a gland and carried in the blood, which alter the activities of their specific target organs

target organs: organs whose activity is altered by a hormone

Exercise 12.7

IN THIS EXERCISE YOU WILL:

- check that you know the vocabulary for this topic
- describe the effects of adrenaline
- compare the way that the nervous system and the endocrine (hormonal) system bring about control and coordination.

Focus

10 Draw *one* line to match each name with its description.

Name	Description
hormone	a hormone secreted by the testes
target organ	a chemical substance produced by an endocrine gland and carried in the blood
insulin	a part of the body that is affected by a hormone
ovaries	organs that secrete oestrogen
testosterone	a hormone secreted by the pancreas

Practice

Adrenaline is secreted when we are nervous.

11 Name the glands that secrete adrenaline.

....

12 Outline the effects of adrenaline.

....

....

....

....

Challenge

13 Complete the table, to compare control and coordination by nerves and by hormones.

Feature	Control by nerves	Control by hormones
how information is transmitted between different parts of the body		
speed of action		
duration of effect		

> Coordination in plants

> **KEY WORDS**
>
> **auxin:** a plant hormone made in the tips of shoots, which causes cells to elongate
>
> **gravitropism:** a response in which part of a plant grows towards or away from gravity
>
> **phototropism:** a response in which part of a plant grows towards or away from the direction from which light is coming
>
> **tropism:** a growth response by a plant, in which the direction of growth is related to the direction of the stimulus

Exercise 12.8

IN THIS EXERCISE YOU WILL:

- think about phototropism and gravitropism
- practise plotting a graph with two lines, using best-fit lines

> use a set of experimental results, and your own knowledge, to provide an explanation.

Focus

A plant growing in a pot was placed on its side, with light coming equally from all directions. Figure 12.6 shows the appearance of the plant after three days.

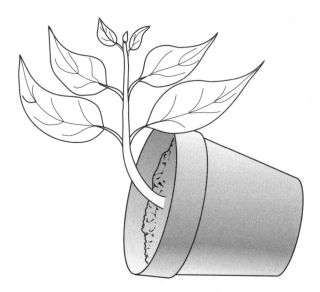

Figure 12.6: A plant growing in a pot that has been placed on its side.

14 The response shown by the shoot of the plant is known as negative gravitropism. Explain what is meant by the term *negative gravitropism*.

....

....

....

15 Explain how we know that this response is gravitropism, not phototropism.

....

....

....

Practice

16 A scientist measured the concentration of a plant hormone, auxin, in the upper and lower surfaces of the plant shoot shown in Figure 12.6. She also measured the percentage increase in length of the upper and lower surface of the plant shoot over a period of one hour.

Tables 12.1 and 12.2 show her results.

	Upper surface	Lower surface
Concentration of auxin / arbitrary units	1.0	1.4

Table 12.1: Concentration of auxin in upper and lower surfaces of the shoot.

Time / minutes	Percentage increase in length	
	Upper surface	Lower surface
10	0.9	1.1
20	1.1	2.2
30	1.6	3.8
40	2.0	5.3
50	2.3	6.6
60	2.8	7.6

Table 12.2: Percentage increase in length of shoot over one hour.

On the grid, draw line graphs to show the results in Table 12.2. Draw both lines on the same set of axes. Draw best-fit lines for each set of results.

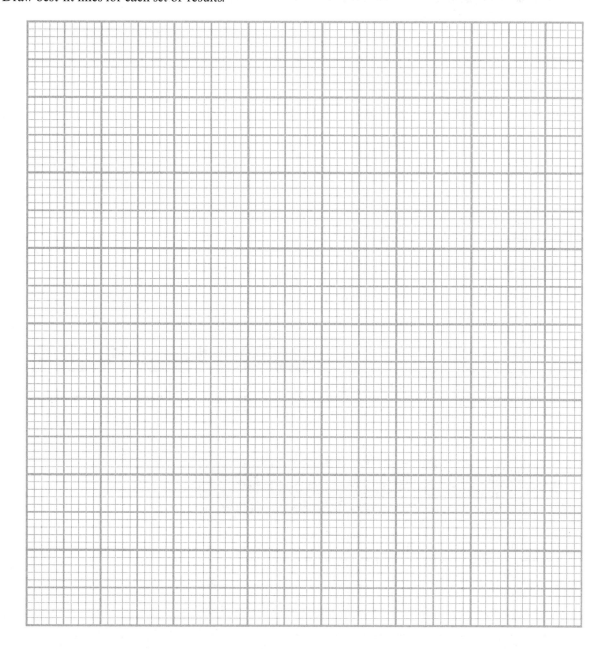

How well did you draw the graph? Give yourself a mark for each of the points in the checklist. Award yourself:

2 marks if you did it well

1 mark if you made a good attempt at it and partly succeeded

0 marks if you did not try to do it, or did not succeed

Checklist	Marks awarded
The axes are labelled fully, with units for the x-axis.	
The scales on both axes take up more than half of the grid, and they go up in even intervals.	
I used a sharp pencil for drawing each cross.	
Each cross is small and neat, and in exactly the right place.	
I used a sharp pencil and ruler to draw both lines.	
The best-fit lines have approximately equal numbers of points above and below them.	
The two lines are labelled to show which set of results they represent, or there is a key.	
Total (out of 14):	

Challenge

17 Use the results in Tables 12.1 and 12.2 to explain what made the plant shoot grow upwards after the pot was turned onto its side.

....

....

....

....

....

....

Excretion and homeostasis

> Excretion

Exercise 13.1

IN THIS EXERCISE YOU WILL:

- check that you remember information about the blood system and the structure of the excretory system

- apply your understanding of diffusion and partially permeable membranes in a new situation.

Focus

Figure 13.1 shows the human excretory system.

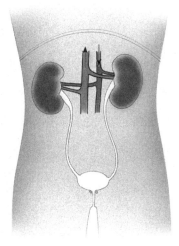

Figure 13.1: The human excretory system.

1   Label these structures on Figure 13.1.

aorta   bladder   kidney   renal artery   renal vein

ureter   urethra   vena cava

> **TIP**
>
> Remember to use a ruler to draw label lines, and make sure that the line touches the structure you want to label.

2   On Figure 13.1, draw arrows in each of the following structures to show the direction in which the liquids inside them flow.

renal artery   renal vein   ureter   urethra

Practice

3   Describe *three* ways in which the liquid contained in the ureter differs from the liquid contained in the renal artery.

> **TIP**
>
> Make sure that your answer describes *differences* between the two liquids. It is usually a good idea to use comparative words, such as 'more' or 'less'.

i   ....

ii   ....

iii   ....

Challenge

If a person's kidneys fail, they may be able to use a kidney dialysis machine to carry out the function of the kidneys.

Figure 13.2 shows how kidney dialysis can be carried out.

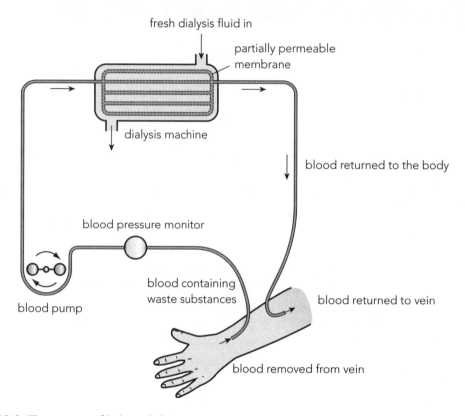

Figure 13.2: The process of kidney dialysis.

4   Suggest why the blood flows through many small channels in the dialysis unit, rather than through a single large channel.

    ....

    ....

5   Table 13.1 shows the concentrations of some of the substances in dialysis fluid and in a person's blood plasma before it enters the dialysis unit. (Don't worry if you are not familiar with the units in the table – you can still answer all the questions!)

Substance	Concentration in dialysis fluid / mmol per dm³	Concentration in blood plasma / mmol per dm³
glucose	5	5
protein	0	8
urea	0	7

Table 13.1: Concentrations of some substances in dialysis fluid and in blood plasma.

Use the information in the table, and your knowledge of diffusion and partially permeable membranes, to answer the following questions.

a   What will happen to the concentration of *glucose* in the person's blood as it passes through the dialysis unit? Explain your answer.

....

....

....

b   What will happen to the concentration of *protein* in the person's blood as it passes through the dialysis unit? Explain your answer.

....

....

....

c   What will happen to the concentration of *urea* in the person's blood as it passes through the dialysis unit? Explain your answer.

....

....

....

PEER ASSESSMENT

Exchange your answers to **5 a–c** with a partner.

Look at your partner's answers. Rate their answers according to the following scheme for each of the questions in the checklist. Award them:

Green   if they did it really well

Amber   if they made a good attempt at it and partly succeeded

Red   if they did not try to do it, or did not succeed

Give feedback to your partner. Tell them *two* things that they have done well, and *one* thing that they could improve.

Checklist	Answer		Colour
Have they clearly stated what will happen?	5	a	
	5	b	
	5	c	
How good do you think their explanation is?	5	a	
	5	b	
	5	c	

Now that you have seen someone else's answers, how do you think that you could improve your own?

....

....

....

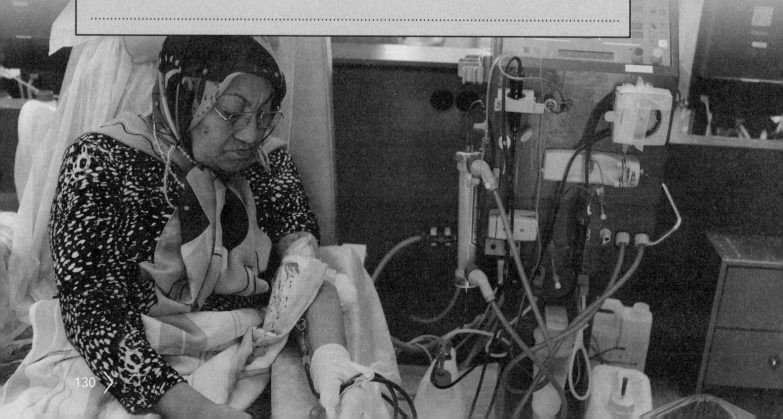

› Homeostasis

KEY WORDS

insulin: a hormone secreted by the pancreas, which decreases blood glucose concentration

negative feedback: a mechanism that detects a move away from the set point, and brings about actions that take the value back towards the set point

set point: the normal value, or range of values, for a particular parameter – for example, the normal range of blood glucose concentration, or the normal body temperature

type 1 diabetes: a condition in which insufficient insulin is secreted by the pancreas, so that blood glucose concentration is not controlled

Exercise 13.2

IN THIS EXERCISE YOU WILL:

- recall information about insulin and its functions
- interpret information presented on a graph
- explain the concept of negative feedback in relation to blood glucose concentration.

Focus

In some people, the control of blood glucose concentration does not work correctly. In type 1 diabetes, insulin is not secreted.

6   Name the gland that normally secretes insulin.

   ....

7   In what circumstances does this gland normally secrete insulin?

   ....

   ....

Practice

The graph in Figure 13.3 shows the concentration of glucose in the blood of two people, after they had eaten a meal containing starch at time 0. One person had type 1 diabetes, and the other did not.

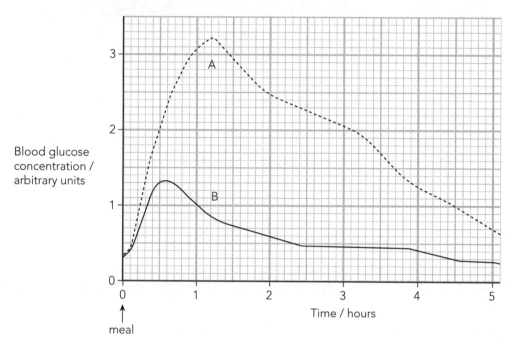

Figure 13.3: Graph showing the concentration of glucose in the blood of two people, A and B.

8   Explain why the concentration of glucose in the blood increases when a person has eaten a meal containing starch.

....

....

....

....

....

....

9   Suggest which person, **A** or **B**, has type 1 diabetes. Explain your answer fully.

....

....

....

....

....

....

....

10   Explain why it is important to keep the concentration of glucose in the blood neither too high nor too low.

....

....

....

....

....

....

....

Challenge

11   Explain how negative feedback and a set point are involved in the control of blood glucose concentration.

....

....

....

....

....

....

Chapter 14

Reproduction in flowering plants

> Asexual and sexual reproduction

KEY WORDS
asexual reproduction: a process resulting in the production of genetically identical offspring from one parent
diploid: having two complete sets of chromosomes
gamete: a sex cell; a cell with half the normal number of chromosomes, whose nucleus fuses with the nucleus of another gamete during sexual reproduction
haploid: having only a single set of chromosomes
sexual reproduction: a process involving the fusion of two gametes to form a zygote and the production of offspring that are genetically different from each other
zygote: a cell that is formed by the fusion of two gametes

Exercise 14.1

IN THIS EXERCISE YOU WILL:

check that you understand the differences between asexual and sexual reproduction.

Focus

1   Complete the table by putting a tick (✓) or cross (✗) into each box.

Feature	Asexual reproduction	Sexual reproduction
always only one parent		
offspring are genetically identical		
gametes are involved		
a zygote is produced		

Practice

2   What are the male and female gametes in a flowering plant?

....

3   What are the male and female gametes in a mammal?

....

4   Figure 14.1 shows a plant reproducing.

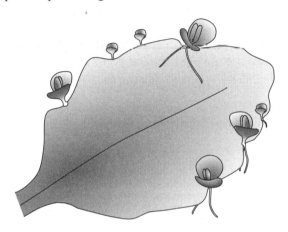

Figure 14.1: A plant reproducing.

Explain why this is an example of asexual reproduction.

....

....

....

Challenge

5   Explain why the nuclei of gametes must be haploid.

....

....

....

....

> Sexual reproduction in flowering plants

Exercise 14.2

IN THIS EXERCISE YOU WILL:

- practise describing what is shown in a graph
- use your knowledge and understanding to make suggestions about an unfamiliar context.

Focus

6   Creeping bent-grass, like almost all grasses, is wind-pollinated.

In the descriptions below, circle the one in each pair that you would expect to describe creeping bent-grass flowers and their pollen.

brightly coloured petals / dull or no petals

anthers dangling outside flower / anthers inside flower

stigma inside flower / feathery stigma outside flower

small quantities of pollen / large quantities of pollen

Practice

The graph in Figure 14.2 shows the quantity of pollen emitted by creeping bent-grass at different times of day, for three days in June and July.

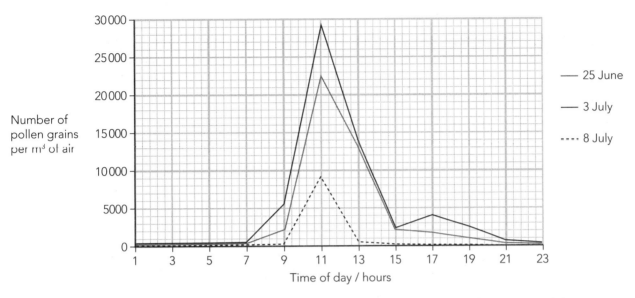

Figure 14.2: A graph showing the quantity of pollen emitted by creeping bent-grass at different times of day.

7   Describe how pollen emission from creeping bent-grass varies during one day.

....

....

....

....

Challenge

8   Describe what will happen in a grass flower, after a pollen grain has landed on a stigma.

....

....

....

....

....

....

> Advantages and disadvantages of different types of reproduction

Exercise 14.3

IN THIS EXERCISE YOU WILL:

- bring together information from different topics

- apply your knowledge and understanding in an unfamiliar context.

Read the information about coffee trees.

Coffee trees are grown to produce their seeds, called coffee beans, which are used all over the world to make coffee drinks and other products. Two species of coffee trees are grown for the commercial production of coffee – *Coffea arabica* and *Coffea canephora*.

Coffee trees normally reproduce by producing seeds. They have flowers with white petals and a very pleasant scent.

Growers can also produce new coffee trees by taking cuttings. This involves cutting a piece from a stem, and placing the lower end in soil. This will then grow roots and eventually grow into a new tree.

Focus

9 Name the genus to which coffee trees belong.

....

10 Use the information to determine whether coffee trees are insect-pollinated or wind-pollinated. Explain your answer.

....

....

11 Name the type of reproduction that is used when a grower produces new coffee trees using cuttings.

....

Practice

12 Would you expect *Coffea arabica* and *Coffea canephora* to be able to reproduce with each other? Explain your answer.

....

....

....

13 Outline the events that must happen in a flower of *Coffea arabica*, before fertilisation can take place.

> **TIP**
>
> 'Outline' means state the main events, briefly. So you need to identify what these are, and then give a concise answer that does not include too much detail.

....

....

....

....

....

Challenge

14 Imagine that you are a coffee grower. A fungal disease called coffee rust has recently begun to attack some of your *Coffea arabica* trees. Some of them seem to be resistant to the fungus and survive, while others are badly damaged. The trees also vary in the quality of the coffee beans that they produce.

Use your understanding of the advantages and disadvantages of different methods of reproduction, to suggest ways in which you might be able to produce a large number of coffee trees that are able to survive attack by coffee rust.

....

....

....

....

....

....

....

....

PEER ASSESSMENT

Exchange your answer with a partner.

Compare your ideas.

Which ideas have you both thought of? Are there any ideas that your partner thought of, but that you did not?

Give feedback to your partner. Tell them *two* things that they have done well, and *one* thing that could be improved.

> Chapter 15

Reproduction in humans

> The human reproductive system

KEY WORDS

acrosome: a structure containing digestive enzymes, in the head of a sperm cell

fetus: an unborn mammal, in which all the organs have been formed

flagellum (plural **flagella**): a long, whip-like 'tail' structure found on sperm cells, used for swimming

placenta: an organ that connects the growing fetus to its mother, in which the blood of the fetus and mother are brought close together so that materials can be exchanged between them

---

Exercise 15.1

IN THIS EXERCISE YOU WILL:

- check that you understand how the structures of egg and sperm cells are related to their functions

- bring together knowledge from several areas of the syllabus to think about transfer of substances from one part of an organism to another.

Focus

Figure 15.1 shows diagrams of human female and male gametes.

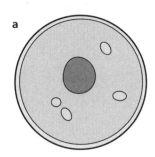

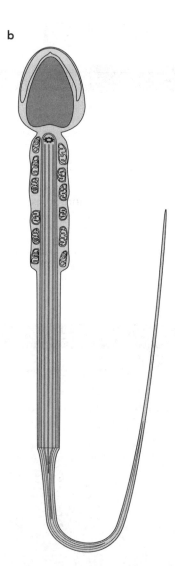

Figure 15.1 a: Human female gamete. **b:** Human male gamete.

1   Use black or dark blue to label all the structures on each gamete that you would find in any animal cell.

Practice

2   Use red or another contrasting colour to label all the structures on each gamete that are adaptations for their specialised functions. Explain how each feature that you label helps the cell to perform its function.

Challenge

The placenta is an organ that allows a mother's blood and her fetus's blood to be brought very closely together, without mixing. Substances are exchanged by diffusion between the two blood systems.

The lungs also contain surfaces where substances are exchanged by diffusion. (This is not the case in the fetus, whose lungs do not function until after it is born.)

Table 15.1 shows some features of the placenta and the lungs in a human.

Feature	Placenta	Lungs
total surface area / m²	16	55
thickness of the barrier across which substances must diffuse / μm	3.5	0.5
approximate rate of blood flow / cm³ per minute	500	5000

Table 15.1: Some features of the human placenta and lungs.

3   Explain how the structure of the lungs provides the large surface area shown in the table.

....

....

....

4   Oxygen moves by diffusion across the exchange surface in both the placenta and the lungs.

   a   State precisely where oxygen moves to and from in the lungs.

....

....

   b   Explain fully why the net movement of oxygen is in this direction in the lungs.

....

....

....

....

5   Use the data in Table 15.1, and your knowledge of the features of gas exchange surfaces, to explain why more oxygen can be absorbed per minute across the lungs than across the placenta.

> **TIP**
>
> This is tricky, so organise your answer on a piece of scrap paper first, before you begin to write. Refer to all three sets of figures in Table 15.1 in your answer.

....

....

....

....

....

....

....

....

6   Oxygen is not the only substance that crosses the placenta from the mother's blood to the fetus's blood.

Amino acids move across the membranes of the cells in the placenta by active transport.

Explain how active transport differs from diffusion.

....

....

....

....

⟩ Sexually transmitted infections

Exercise 15.2

Focus

The United Nations set a target that, by 2020:

- 90% of people living with HIV would know that they have the virus

- 90% of all people diagnosed with HIV infection would receive antiretroviral drugs

- 90% of all people receiving antiretroviral drugs would have the activity of the virus in their bodies suppressed (that is, they would not develop AIDS).

Table 15.2 shows the percentage of people in Asia and the Pacific region who are infected with HIV, who knew that they had the virus.

Year	Percentage of people living with HIV who knew they had the virus
2015	59
2016	62
2017	65
2018	65

Table 15.2: Data about HIV in the Asia and Pacific region.

7 On the grid below, draw a bar chart to display these data.

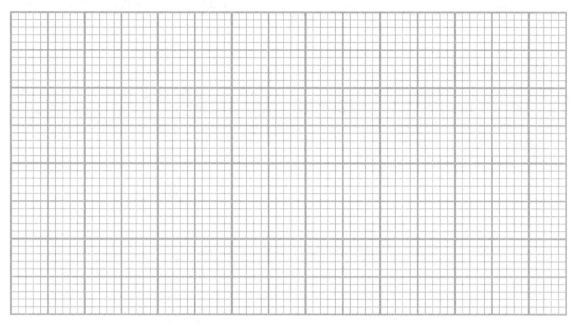

Practice

8 Suggest how the data in Table 15.2 have been estimated.

....

....

....

....

....

Challenge

9 Table 15.3 shows data relating to the other two components of the United Nations' target.

Year	Percentage of people diagnosed with HIV who are receiving antiretroviral drugs	Percentage of people receiving antiretroviral drugs in whom the virus is suppressed
2015	62	89
2016	68	89
2017	74	90
2018	79	90

Table 15.3: Data relating to the other two components of the United Nations' target.

Use all the data to discuss the progress made by the United Nations in achieving its target in the Asia and Pacific region. Use the data to evaluate the likelihood that the target will be achieved by 2020.

> **TIP**
>
> When you are asked to 'discuss', you are expected to give two sides of an argument. In this case, you should be able to describe some ways in which progress is being made, but also some points suggesting why the target might not be met.

....

....

....

....

....

....

....

....

....

....

....

SELF-ASSESSMENT

How well do you think you answered question **9**? Rate your success for each of the questions in the checklist, using:

Green if you did it well

Amber if you made a good attempt at it and partly succeeded

Red if you did not try to do it, or did not succeed

Did you ...	Colour
clearly state whether you think the target will be achieved?	
make some points describing the progress that is being made, and some that suggest that the target might not be met?	
quote data from the table to support each statement that you made?	

Chapter 16

Inheritance

> Chromosomes and cell division

KEY WORDS

chromosome: a length of DNA, found in the nucleus of a cell; it contains genetic information in the form of many different genes

gene: a length of DNA that codes for one protein

> **meiosis:** division of a diploid nucleus resulting in four genetically different haploid nuclei; this is sometimes called a reduction division

> **mitosis:** division of a cell nucleus resulting in two genetically identical nuclei (i.e. with the same number and kind of chromosomes as the parent nucleus)

Exercise 16.1

IN THIS EXERCISE YOU WILL:

* review your understanding of chromosomes

> check that you understand the differences between mitosis and meiosis.

Focus

Figure 16.1 shows a chromosome, just before the cell it is part of divides.

Figure 16.1: A chromosome just before cell division.

---

1   State the part of a cell in which chromosomes are found.

    ....

2   Name the chemical that contains genetic information and that is found in chromosomes.

    ....

3   Chromosomes contain genes. What is a gene?

    ....

    ....

Practice

Cell M is a cell in the body of an animal. It contains two sets of chromosomes. Each set is made up of 16 chromosomes.

4   a   What is the term for a cell that contains two complete sets of chromosomes?

        ....

    b   How many chromosomes will be present in a gamete produced by this animal?

        ....

5   The cell divides by mitosis to produce cells P and Q.

    a   How many chromosomes are there in cell P?

        ....

    b   Are cells P and Q genetically different, or genetically identical to the parent cell?

        ....

    c   List *three* roles of mitosis in plants and animals.

        i   ....

        ii   ....

        iii ....

Challenge

6 Cell M now divides by meiosis.

Outline *three* differences between the outcome of this division, and the division by mitosis described in question **5**.

> **TIP**
>
> When you are asked to outline differences, you can do this in the form of a table if you find it easier than writing sentences.

i ....

ii ....

iii ....

> Inheriting genes

> **KEY WORDS**
>
> **alleles:** alternative forms of a gene
>
> **dominant allele:** an allele that is expressed if it is present (e.g. **G**)
>
> **genetic diagram:** a standard way of showing all the steps in making predictions about the probable genotypes and phenotypes of the offspring from two parents
>
> **genotype:** the genetic makeup of an organism in terms of the alleles present (e.g. **GG**)
>
> **heterozygous:** having two different alleles of a particular gene (e.g. **Gg**)
>
> **homozygous:** having two identical alleles of a particular gene (e.g. **GG** or **gg**)
>
> **phenotype:** the observable features of an organism
>
> **recessive allele:** an allele that is only expressed when there is no dominant allele of the gene present (e.g. **g**)
>
> **sex-linked genes:** genes that are found on a part of one of the sex chromosomes (usually the X chromosome) and not on the other sex chromosome; they therefore produce characteristics that are more common in one sex than in the other

Exercise 16.2: Focus

IN THIS EXERCISE YOU WILL:

- revise your knowledge of classification

- practise using a genetic diagram.

Fruit flies, *Drosophila melanogaster*, are often used for research into genetics. Figure 16.2 shows a fruit fly.

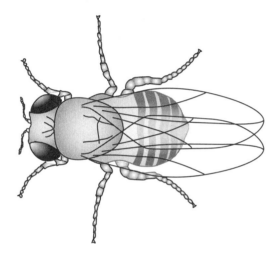

Figure 16.2: A fruit fly, *Drosophila melanogaster*.

7   State *three* features, visible in Figure 16.2, that show that the fruit fly is an insect.

> **TIP**
>
> Make sure that features you state are visible in the diagram – not other features of insects that are not shown.

i   ....

ii   ....

iii   ....

8   What is the genus of the fruit fly?

....

9 Fruit flies can have normal wings or vestigial (really small) wings. The allele for normal wings, **N**, is dominant. The allele for vestigial wings, **n**, is recessive.

Complete the table to show the possible genotypes and phenotypes for fruit fly wings. Be very careful to write the letters **N** and **n** so that there is no doubt whether each one is a capital letter or a small letter.

Genotype	Phenotype

10 Complete the genetic diagram to predict the genotypes and phenotypes of the offspring of a heterozygous normal-winged fly and a vestigial-winged fly.

phenotypes of parents   normal wings   vestigial wings

genotypes of parent   ....

gametes   ◯ and ◯   all ◯

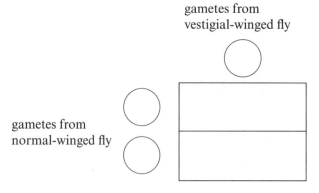

gametes from
vestigial-winged fly

gametes from
normal-winged fly

11 The two flies had 82 offspring.

Predict approximately how many of these would have vestigial wings.

....

....

Exercise 16.3: Practice

The family tree (pedigree) in Figure 16.3 shows the incidence of a genetic disease called PKU in four generations of a family.

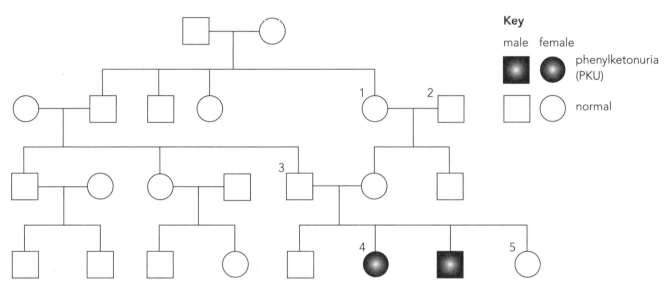

Figure 16.3: A family tree showing incidence of PKU.

12 Describe *one* piece of evidence from the diagram that suggests PKU is caused by a recessive allele.

....

....

....

13 If PKU is caused by a recessive allele, explain why it is unlikely that this allele first appeared in person 4.

....

....

....

....

14 In the space below, deduce the possible genotypes of persons 1, 2, 3 and 4. Use the symbol **q** for the PKU allele and the symbol **Q** for the normal allele.

....

....

....

....

....

15 Person 5 is worried that her children might have PKU. She talks to a genetic counsellor. What might she be told?

....

....

....

....

....

....

Exercise 16.4: Challenge

IN THIS EXERCISE YOU WILL:

apply your understanding of sex linkage to a new situation.

In fruit flies, as in humans, males have an X and a Y chromosome, and females have two X chromosomes.

There is a gene on the X chromosome that affects eye colour. The dominant allele of this gene produces red eyes, and the recessive allele produces white eyes.

16 Suggest suitable symbols for the two alleles of this gene.

....

17 In the space below, construct a genetic diagram to predict the ratios of eye colour in male and female offspring of a white-eyed male fly and a heterozygous red-eyed female fly.

....

....

....

Exchange your genetic diagram with a partner. Rate their diagram for each of the points in the checklist, using:

Green if they did it really well

Amber if they made a good attempt at it and partly succeeded

Red if they did not try to do it, or did not succeed

Checklist	Colour
Is it easy to follow your partner's genetic diagram?	
Have they written the full headings for each row?	
Have they drawn circles around the gamete genotypes?	
Have they clearly shown the phenotypes produced by each genotype in the offspring?	
Have they clearly stated the ratios of phenotypes that they predict?	

Give feedback to your partner. Tell them *two* things that they have done well, and *one* thing that could be improved.

> Genes and protein synthesis

DNA: a molecule that contains genetic information, in the form of genes, that control the proteins that are made in the cell

expressed: used to make a protein; a gene is expressed when the protein that it codes for is synthesised in a cell

messenger RNA (mRNA): a molecule that carries a copy of the information on DNA to a ribosome, to be used to synthesise a protein

stem cells: unspecialised cells that are able to divide by mitosis to produce different types of specialised cell

Exercise 16.5

IN THIS EXERCISE YOU WILL:

• practise using correct terminology about genes and protein synthesis

• think about why not all cells express the same genes.

Focus

18 Choose suitable words to complete these sentences.

A .... is a length of DNA that codes for the production of a protein.

The sequence of .... in a gene determines the sequence of ....

in the protein that is made.

Proteins are synthesised on the .... in the cytoplasm of a cell. A copy of the

gene is carried to the cytoplasm by a molecule called ....

Practice

19 Name *two* types of protein whose function depends on the precise shape of the molecule.

i ....

ii ....

20 Explain why a change in the structure of a DNA molecule could result in the loss of function of these types of proteins.

....

....

....

....

Challenge

Stem cells are unspecialised cells that are able to divide by mitosis and produce new cells that become specialised for different functions.

21 State how the genes contained in the specialised cells differ, if at all, from the genes contained in the stem cells.

....

....

22 Explain what happens to the genes in a cell, as it becomes specialised for its specific function.

....

....

....

....

....

....

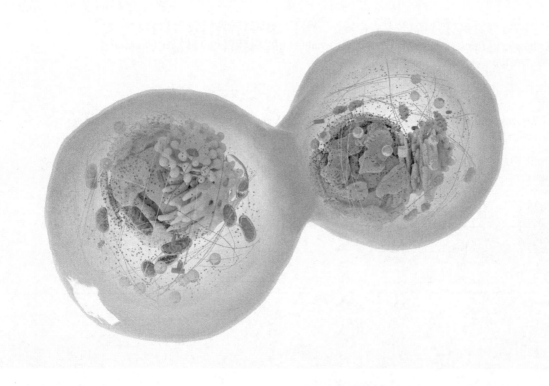

> Chapter 17

Variation and selection

> Variation

KEY WORDS

adaptive feature: an inherited feature that helps an organism to survive and reproduce in its environment

continuous variation: variation in which there is a continuous range of phenotypes between two extremes

discontinuous variation: variation in which there are distinct categories of phenotype, with no intermediates

hydrophyte: a plant that has adaptive features that help it to survive in water

Exercise 17.1

IN THIS EXERCISE YOU WILL:

- use data to plot a histogram
- calculate a magnification

> apply your knowledge of adaptations of hydrophytes in a new situation.

Focus

Water hyacinths are aquatic plants that originally came from Brazil, but now grow in waterways in many tropical countries.

A researcher collected 30 water hyacinth plants from a river. She measured the mass of each plant. Table 17.1 shows her results.

Mass range / kg	0.5–0.9	1.0–1.4	1.5–1.9	2.0–2.4	2.5–2.9	3.0–3.4
Number of plants	1	3	8	9	7	2

Table 17.1: A results table.

1   Does the mass of water hyacinth plants show continuous variation or discontinuous variation? Explain your answer.

    ....

    ....

    ....

2   Plot a histogram (frequency diagram) to display the data in the table.

TIP
Remember that the bars should touch in a histogram.

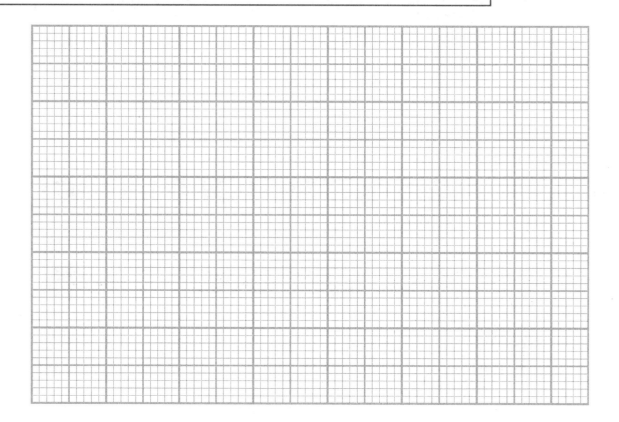

Practice

Water hyacinths are sometimes used to help to clean up polluted water, because they are able to take up pollutants such as heavy metals.

An experiment carried out in China investigated differences in the structure of the leaf epidermis of water hyacinth plants grown in clean water and in polluted water.

Figure 17.1 and Table 17.2 show some of their results.

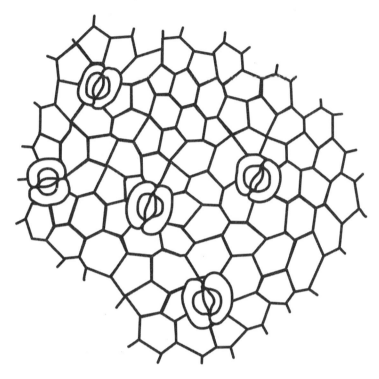

Figure 17.1: Upper epidermis of a water hyacinth leaf grown in polluted water.

Type of water	Upper or lower epidermis	Mean width of stomatal pore / μm	Mean length of guard cell / μm	Mean number of stomata per mm²
clean	upper	4	7	2.83
	lower	4	7	3.32
polluted	upper	3	5	2.80
	lower	3	5	2.83

Table 17.2: Differences in features of leaf epidermis of hyacinths grown in clean and polluted water.

3   State the mean length of a guard cell in the upper epidermis of a water hyacinth leaf grown in polluted water.

....

4 **a** Measure the length, in mm, of a guard cell in Figure 17.1.

..................mm

b Convert your answer in mm to an answer in μm. 1 mm = 1000 μm.

..................μm

c Use your answers to **3** and **4b** to calculate the magnification of the diagram. Write down the formula that you use, and show your working.

....

Challenge

5 Explain how the results in Table 17.2 for water hyacinth leaves grown in clean water suggest that this plant is adapted for growing in water.

....

....

....

....

....

....

....

6 Compare the characteristics of the leaf epidermis of the plants growing in clean water with plants growing in polluted water.

....

....

....

....

....

〉 Selection

Exercise 17.2: Focus

IN THIS EXERCISE YOU WILL:

check how well you understand the process of natural selection and that you can use suitable terms to describe it.

7   Choose the best words from the list to complete the sentences about natural selection.

> alleles   community   compete   environment   fewer   generation
>
> individuals   more   reproduce   species   survive   variation

Natural selection depends on the fact that there is .... within populations.

In most populations, far .... young are produced than will live long enough

to be able to .... The organisms in the population have to ....

for scarce resources.

As a result, only the .... that are best adapted to their .... are

likely to have offspring. Their .... are the ones that are most likely to be passed

on to the next ....

Exercise 17.3: Practice

IN THIS EXERCISE YOU WILL:

- practise describing the information shown in a graph

> apply your understanding of the development of antibiotic resistance in bacteria to a new situation.

Cotton is a crop that is grown to produce fibres to make cloth. Cotton bollworms are insect pests of cotton plants. Growers use insecticides to try to reduce their losses from these pests.

The graph in Figure 17.2 shows the frequency of resistance of cotton bollworms to an insecticide that was commonly used in Australia, between 1997 and 2002.

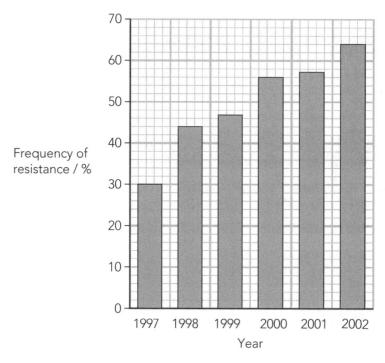

Figure 17.2: Graph showing the frequency of resistance of cotton bollworms to an insecticide.

8   Describe the change in the frequency of resistance to the insecticide over this time period.

....

....

....

....

9   Using your knowledge of the development of resistance to antibiotics in bacteria, explain how the development of resistance to insecticides could have occurred.

....

....

....

....

....

....

....

....

....

....

....

Exercise 17.4: Challenge

IN THIS EXERCISE YOU WILL:

- practise comparing two sets of information shown in a graph

- apply your understanding of selective breeding to a new situation.

In the second half of the 20th century, a group of cows were put into a selective breeding programme, to try to increase the milk yield over several generations. A control group was also used, in which selective breeding was not carried out.

The graph in Figure 17.3 shows the changes in milk yield over a 35-year period. The values plotted show the mean milk yield of all the cows born in a particular year.

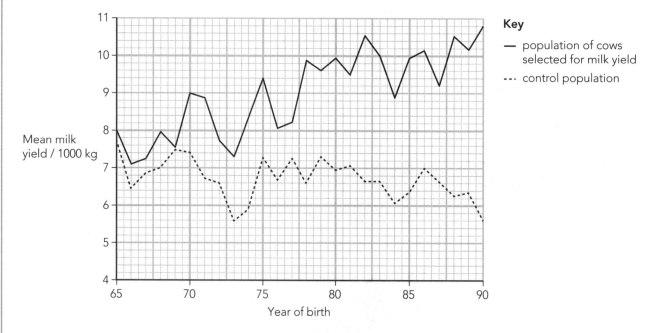

Figure 17.3: Graph showing the changes in milk yield over a 35-year period.

10 Compare the change in milk yield for the population of cows selected for milk yield, with the control population.

> **TIP**
>
> It would be good to plan your answer before you begin to write. Make a list of the points you would like to make – for example, the general trends, any particular years that stand out, data quotes for particular years, and a calculation such as the difference between the two populations in one year or the overall changes for the two populations.

....

....

....

....

....

....

....

....

....

....

11 Suggest explanations for the differences that you describe in your answer to **10**.

....

....

....

....

....

....

....

....

....

....

....

> Chapter 18

Organisms and their environment

> Energy flow and food webs

KEY WORDS

community: all of the populations of all the different species in an ecosystem

ecosystem: a unit containing all of the organisms in a community and their environment, interacting together

food chain: a diagram showing the transfer of energy from one organism to the next, beginning with a producer

food web: a network of interconnected food chains

trophic level: the position of an organism in a food chain, food web or ecological pyramid

Exercise 18.1

IN THIS EXERCISE YOU WILL:

- use information to construct a food chain
- identify trophic levels
- carry out a calculation.

Focus

In a meadow, grass and other plants grow. Mice and voles eat the seeds of the plants. Grasshoppers eat the grass leaves. Spiders eat grasshoppers. The mice are eaten by snakes and foxes. Spiders are eaten by small birds.

1   What is the term used to describe all of the organisms, belonging to all the different species, that live in the meadow?

    ....

2   In the space below, construct a food web to show the feeding relationships in the meadow.

Practice

3 Figure 18.1 shows the energy contained in four trophic levels of a food chain from the meadow. The numbers are in arbitrary units.

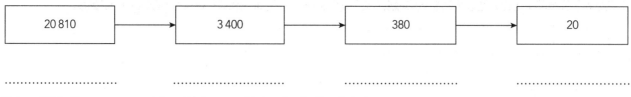

Figure 18.1: The energy contained in four trophic levels of a food chain.

a Explain what is meant by the term *trophic level*.

....

....

b Underneath each box in Figure 18.1, write the correct term for the organisms in that trophic level.

> Challenge

4 **a** Calculate the percentage of energy in the first trophic level that is transferred to the fourth trophic level. Show your working.

....

b Describe where all the rest of the energy goes.

....

....

....

Nutrient cycles

KEY WORDS

nitrification: converting ammonium ions to nitrate ions

nitrogen fixation: converting inert nitrogen gas into a more reactive form, such as nitrate ions or ammonia

Exercise 18.2

IN THIS EXERCISE YOU WILL:

- check your knowledge of the carbon cycle
- apply understanding of the nitrogen cycle to an unfamiliar situation.

Focus

Figure 18.2 shows part of the carbon cycle.

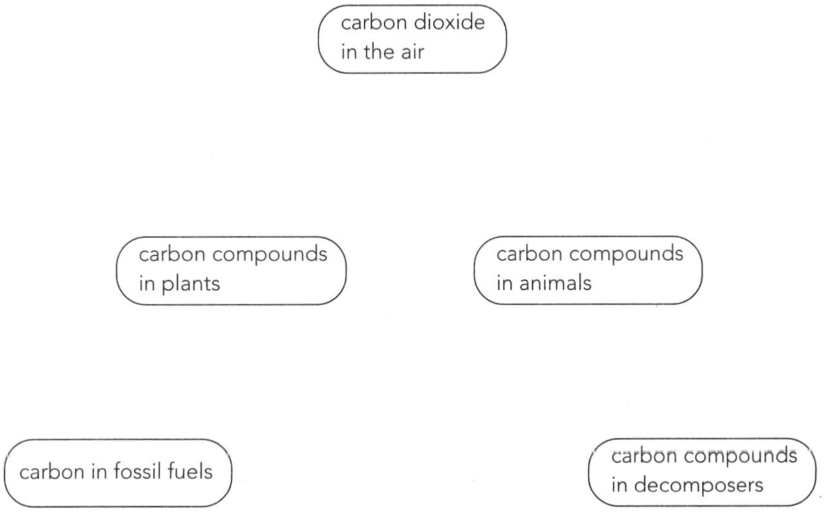

Figure 18.2: Part of the carbon cycle.

5 Complete the diagram by drawing arrows to show how carbon atoms move through the cycle. Label each of your arrows with one of these words. You will need to use at least one of the words more than once.

combustion **feeding** **photosynthesis** **respiration**

Practice

A fish tank was filled with water and some bacteria were added. Some phytoplankton (microscopic plants) were then introduced. The tank was put into a dark place and left for eight months.

At intervals, the water was tested to find out what it contained. The results are shown in the graph (Figure 18.3).

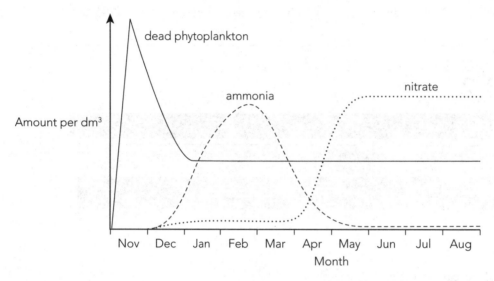

Figure 18.3: Graph showing the amount of phytoplankton, ammonia and nitrate in the water over eight months.

6   Explain why the phytoplankton died so quickly.

    ....

    ....

7   The phytoplankton contained nitrogen in their cells. Name *two* different types of organic compound in cells that contain nitrogen.

    ....

8   Explain why the quantity of dead phytoplankton decreased from mid-November to the end of December.

    ....

    ....

    ....

Challenge

9   The graph shows that, after one month, ammonia began to appear in the water.

Use your knowledge of the nitrogen cycle to explain where this ammonia came from.

....

....

....

10   State the times at which nitrate began to appear in the water, and when its concentration began to increase.

....

....

11   Use your knowledge of the nitrogen cycle to explain where the nitrate came from.

....

....

〉 Populations

KEY WORDS
death phase: the final stage in a population growth curve where the population falls; death rate exceeds birth rate
lag phase: the stage at the start of a population growth curve where the population remains small and grows only very slowly
log phase or **exponential phase:** the stage in a population growth curve where the population grows at its maximum rate; birth rate exceeds death rate
sigmoid growth curve: an S-shaped curve showing the change in the size of a population through all the phases in population growth
stationary phase: the stage in a population growth curve where the population remains roughly constant; birth rate equals death rate

Exercise 18.3

Focus

12 Define the term *population*.

....

....

13 Flour beetles are small beetles that live in and feed on flour. Five flour beetles were placed in a container of flour. The beetles were counted at regular intervals over the next 900 days.

The results are shown in Figure 18.4.

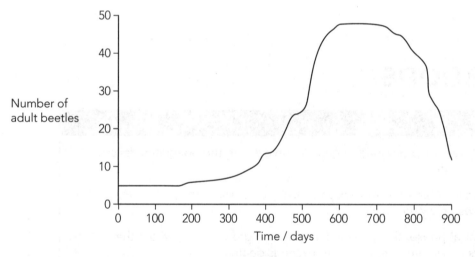

Figure 18.4: Sigmoid growth curve of a population of flour beetles.

On the graph, label these phases:

lag phase   log (exponential) phase   stationary phase   death phase

Practice

14 Write the name of the phase or phases where:

    a   the death rate is greater than the birth rate

    ....

    b   the birth rate is greater than the death rate

    ....

    c   the birth rate and the death rate are equal.

    ....

15 Suggest a reason for the shape of the curve between 600 days and 900 days.

....

....

Challenge

16 The experiment was repeated, but some beetles of another species, which also eat flour, were added at the same time as the five flour beetles of the original species.

    a   On the graph in Figure 18.4, sketch a curve to predict the population changes in the size of the original species of flour beetles in this new experiment.

    b   Explain your predictions.

> **TIP**
>
> Try to ensure that your answers explain *all* of the differences between the line you have sketched and the original line.

....

....

....

....

....

Chapter 19

Human influences on ecosystems

> Human pressures on ecosystems

Exercise 19.1

IN THIS EXERCISE YOU WILL:

use data to draw conclusions about methods of livestock farming.

Focus

A study was carried out into farming methods on a small pineapple farm in Uganda. The farmers kept livestock as well as growing pineapples.

The graph in Figure 19.1 shows how cattle, goats and chickens were fed on the pineapple farm.

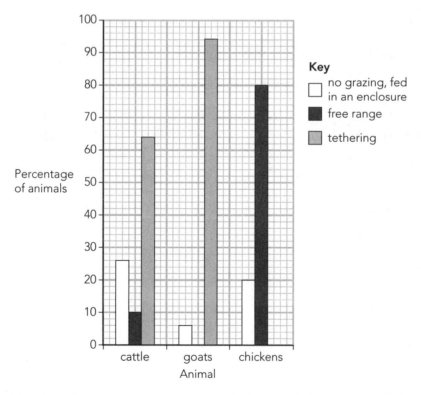

Figure 19.1: A bar chart showing how cattle, goats and chickens are fed on a pineapple farm.

1   State the feeding method that was most commonly used for cattle.

....

2   Compare the types of feeding methods used for chickens with those used for goats.

....

....

....

Practice

*   Feeding method **A** involved keeping the animals in enclosures all the time. They were fed on waste from the crops produced on the farm, and also on food supplements that were bought by the farmers.

*   Feeding method **B** allowed the animals to move around the farm and graze freely.

*   Feeding method **C** involved tying the animals to a post so that they could graze in a small area. They were moved to a different post from time to time.

3   Which of the three feeding methods could be classified as intensive livestock production? Explain your answer.

....

....

....

....

4   Suggest how keeping livestock could help the farmer to reduce the use of chemical fertilisers for growing pineapples.

> **TIP**
>
> Remember that there may be more than one suitable answer for a 'suggest' question. You need to think about how you can use your knowledge and understanding to provide a good answer to the question.

....

....

....

Challenge

5   Some of the cows kept on these farms were native breeds, which had been developed in the local area. Others were crossbreeds, which had been bred by crossing a cow from the local breed with a bull from a non-native breed.

    a   It is expensive for a farmer to use a non-native bull to cross with her native breed cows. Suggest why some farmers did this.

....

....

....

    b   The scientists who carried out the study found that 78% of the crossbreed cows were infected with parasitic worms, while only 48% of the native breeds were infected.

       Suggest reasons for this difference.

> **TIP**
>
> Note that the question asks for reasons, so you should give at least two different ones.

....

....

....

....

....

〉 Conservation

Exercise 19.2

IN THIS EXERCISE YOU WILL:

apply your understanding of threats to endangered species in a new context.

Focus

Table 19.1 lists four species of mammal in Chile that were considered to be endangered in 1983. It also shows the reasons why each mammal was endangered.

Species	Description of species	Main reason why it is endangered	Other reason why it is endangered
Pudu puda	small deer	loss of habitat	hunting; diseases transferred from introduced species
Ctenomys robustus	burrowing rodent	loss of habitat	
Chinchilla lanigera	burrowing rodent	hunting	loss of habitat
Lutra provocax	otter	hunting	

Table 19.1: Four species of mammals that were endangered in 1983.

6   Explain what the two words in the name of the species tell us about the classification of the species.

....

....

7   State what is meant by an *endangered species*.

....

....

8   Outline *two* reasons why the habitat of a species may be lost.

i   ....

ii   ....

Practice

9 Explain why loss of habitat can cause a species to become endangered.

....

....

....

....

10 *Chinchilla lanigera* and *Lutra provocax* are now protected and are no longer hunted. Despite this, both species are still endangered.

Use the information in Table 19.1 to suggest why, despite the ban on hunting, *C. lanigera* is still endangered.

....

....

> Challenge

11 Introduced animals may carry pathogens which do not threaten them but can be very harmful to native species.

Use your knowledge of the immune response to suggest why animals such as *Pudu puda* may be harmed by diseases transferred from introduced species.

....

....

....

....

....

....

12 Only seven small populations of *L. provocax* are known, and these are all isolated from one another.

Suggest why this species has not been able to increase its numbers significantly, despite being protected.

....

....

....

....

....

....

PEER ASSESSMENT

Exchange your answer to **12** with a partner.

How easy is it to understand the answer they have written?

Are their suggestions the same as yours?

Have they made any good suggestions that you did not think of?

Give feedback to your partner. Tell them *two* things that they have done well, and *one* thing that they could improve.

Chapter 20

Biotechnology and genetic modification

> Biotechnology

> **KEY WORDS**
>
> **fermenter:** a vessel, usually made of steel or glass, in which microorganisms can be grown in order to produce a required product
>
> **pectinase:** an enzyme that is used to digest pectin, increasing the quantity of juice that can be extracted from fruit, and clarifying the juice
>
> **sterilised:** treated – e.g. with steam – to destroy all living cells

Exercise 20.1

IN THIS EXERCISE YOU WILL:

- check your understanding of how pectinase is used
- describe how a fermenter provides controlled conditions for growth of microorganisms
- consider the best way to display a set of data.

Focus

Pectinase is an enzyme that is used in the manufacture of fruit juice. Pectinase is produced by microorganisms, such as the fungus *Penicillium viridicatum*.

1 Pectinase is an enzyme. Explain what is meant by the term *enzyme*.

....

....

....

2 Name the substrate of pectinase.

....

3 Explain why pectinase is used in food production.

....

....

....

....

Practice

Table 20.1 shows the production of pectinase by *P. viridicatum* when it is grown on different kinds of waste material from food processing. Bagasse is the waste material left over from processing sugar cane.

Substrate	Production of pectinase / arbitrary units
wheat bran	1200
mango peel	450
banana peel	75
wheat bran + sugar cane bagasse	1500
mango peel + sugar cane bagasse	1500
banana peel + sugar cane bagasse	1000

Table 20.1: The production of pectinase when it is grown on different kinds of waste material.

4 Display these data on the grid in a way that clearly shows how adding sugar cane bagasse to the substrate affects the production of pectinase.

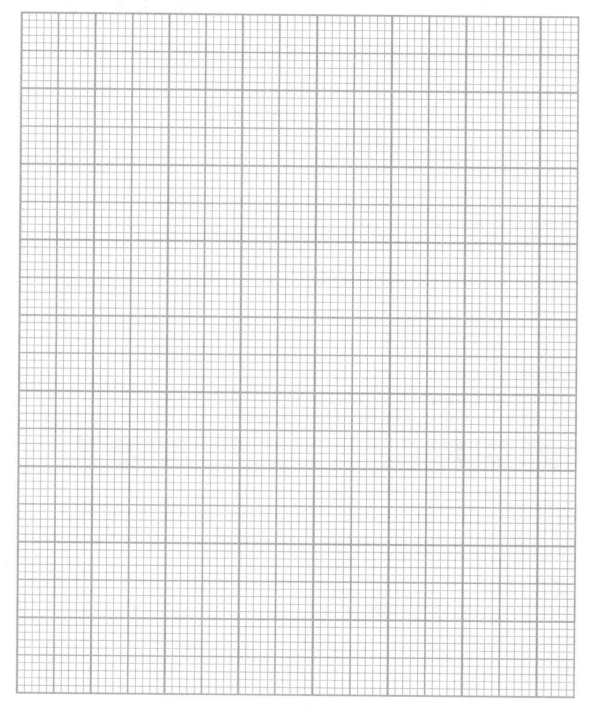

5   Suggest how using food processing waste materials as substrates for the production of pectinase could benefit the environment.

....

....

....

Challenge

6   *P. viridicatum* is grown in fermenters.

a   What is a fermenter?

....

....

b List *three* conditions that are controlled in the fermenter while *P. viridicatum* is growing in it. For each condition, explain why and how it is controlled.

Condition 1 ....

Why it is controlled ....

....

How it is controlled ....

....

Condition 2 ....

Why it is controlled ....

....

How it is controlled ....

....

Condition 3 ....

Why it is controlled ....

....

How it is controlled ....

....

〉 Genetic modification

KEY WORDS

DNA ligase: an enzyme that joins two DNA molecules together

genetic modification: changing the genetic material of an organism by removing, changing or inserting individual genes

recombinant plasmid: a small circle of DNA, found in bacteria, which contains both the bacterial DNA and DNA from a different organism

restriction enzymes: enzymes (biological catalysts) that cut DNA at specific points, and leave a short length of unpaired bases at each end

sticky ends: lengths of unpaired bases on one strand of a DNA molecule; they are able to form bonds with complementary lengths of unpaired bases on a different DNA molecule

Exercise 20.2

IN THIS EXERCISE YOU WILL:

- check that you can give some examples of genetic modification

  〉 apply your knowledge of genetic modification in a new context.

Focus

7   Explain what is meant by the term *genetic modification*.

   ....

   ....

   ....

8   List *three* ways in which crop plants have been genetically modified.

   i   ....

   ii   ....

   iii   ....

Practice

9 Many people in the world do not have enough vitamin A in their diet. We can make vitamin A in the body from carotene, which is found naturally in many plants. Rice has all the genes for making carotene, but some of these genes are turned off in the rice grains.

Researchers have added two genes to rice plants, which code for the production of two enzymes that enable the production of carotene in rice grains. Figure 20.1 shows how one of the genes, from a bacterium, was added.

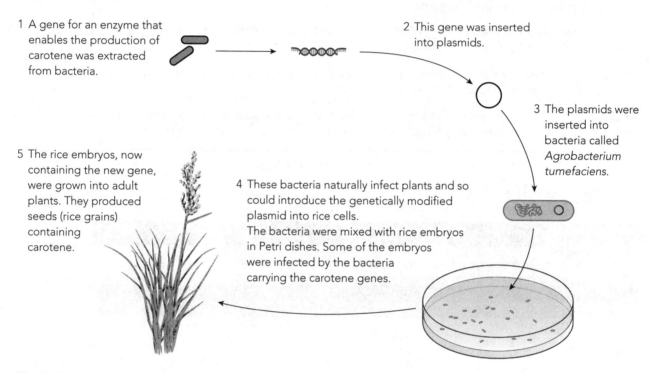

1 A gene for an enzyme that enables the production of carotene was extracted from bacteria.

2 This gene was inserted into plasmids.

3 The plasmids were inserted into bacteria called *Agrobacterium tumefaciens*.

4 These bacteria naturally infect plants and so could introduce the genetically modified plasmid into rice cells.
The bacteria were mixed with rice embryos in Petri dishes. Some of the embryos were infected by the bacteria carrying the carotene genes.

5 The rice embryos, now containing the new gene, were grown into adult plants. They produced seeds (rice grains) containing carotene.

Figure 20.1: Diagram showing how a gene was added to rice plants.

a On Figure 20.1, write the letter **R** at one step at which restriction enzymes would be used.

b Restriction enzymes cut DNA to leave sticky ends.

   i Explain what sticky ends are.

   ....

   ....

   ii Explain why it is useful to cut the DNA so that there are sticky ends.

   ....

   ....

   ....

   ....

c   On Figure 20.1, write the letter **L** to indicate one step at which DNA ligase would be used.

d   Explain the role of plasmids in the process of producing the genetically modified rice.

....

....

....

....

Challenge

10   Use the information in Figure 20.1, and your own knowledge, to explain why *Agrobacterium tumefaciens* was used in this process.

....

....

....

....

11   Suggest why the researchers decided to produce this new form of rice by genetic modification, rather than by selective breeding.

> **TIP**
>
> Think carefully about the differences between selective breeding and genetic modification. You might like to make some brief notes on some spare paper. Then use the information above to help you to think about why genetic modification is more likely to achieve the required result than selective breeding.

....

....

....

....

....

....

....

....

....

> Glossary

absorption: the movement of nutrients from the alimentary canal into the blood

accommodation: changing the shape of the lens to focus on objects at different distances from the eye

acrosome: a structure containing digestive enzymes, in the head of a sperm cell

active immunity: long-term defence against a pathogen by antibody production in the body

active site: the part of an enzyme molecule to which the substrate temporarily binds

active transport: the movement of molecules or ions through a cell membrane from a region of lower concentration to a region of higher concentration (i.e. against a concentration gradient) using energy from respiration

adaptation: the process, resulting from natural selection, by which populations become more suited to their environment over many generations

adaptive feature: an inherited feature that helps an organism to survive and reproduce in its environment

adrenaline: a hormone secreted by the adrenal glands, which prepares the body for fight or flight

aerobic respiration: chemical reactions that take place in mitochondria, which use oxygen to break down glucose and other nutrient molecules to release energy for the cell to use

alleles: alternative forms of a gene

alveoli (singular: **alveolus**): tiny air-filled sacs in the lungs where gas exchange takes place

amino acids: substances with molecules containing carbon, hydrogen, oxygen and nitrogen; there are 20 different amino acids found in organisms

anaerobic respiration: chemical reactions in cells that break down nutrient molecules to release energy, without using oxygen

antagonistic muscles: a pair of muscles whose contraction has opposite effects; when one contracts, the other relaxes

anther: the structure at the top of a stamen, inside which pollen grains are made

antibodies: proteins secreted by white blood cells, which bind to pathogens and help to destroy them

antigen: a chemical that is recognised by the body as being 'foreign' – that is, it is not part of the body's normal set of chemical substances – and stimulates the production of antibodies

aorta: the largest artery in the body, which receives oxygenated blood from the left ventricle and delivers it to the body organs

arbitrary units: these are sometimes used on a graph scale to represent quantitative differences between values, instead of 'real' units such as seconds or centimetres; this is usually because the real units would be very complicated to use

asexual reproduction: a process resulting in the production of genetically identical offspring from one parent

atria: the thin-walled chambers at the top of the heart, which receive blood

auxin: a plant hormone made in the tips of shoots, which causes cells to elongate

axon: a long, thin, fibre of cytoplasm that extends from the cell body of a neurone

bacteria: unicellular organisms whose cells do not contain a nucleus

balanced diet: a diet that contains all of the required nutrients, in suitable proportions, and the right amount of energy

base: one of the components of DNA; there are four bases, A, C, G and T, and their sequence determines the proteins that are made in a cell

Benedict's solution: a blue liquid that turns orange-red when heated with reducing sugar

bile: an alkaline fluid produced by the liver, which helps with fat digestion

bile duct: the tube that carries bile from the gall bladder to the duodenum

binomial system: a system of naming species that is internationally agreed, in which the scientific name is made up of two parts showing the genus and the species

biuret reagent: a blue solution that turns purple when mixed with amino acids or proteins

carbohydrates: substances that include sugars, starch and cellulose; they contain carbon, hydrogen and oxygen

carrier proteins (or **protein carriers**): protein molecules in cell membranes that can use energy to change shape and move ions or molecules into or out of a cell

cell membrane: a very thin layer surrounding the cytoplasm of every cell; it controls what enters and leaves the cell

cell sap: the fluid that fills the large vacuoles in plant cells

cell wall: a tough layer outside the cell membrane; found in the cells of plants, fungi and bacteria

cells: the smallest units from which all organisms are made

cellulose: a carbohydrate that forms long fibres, and makes up the cell walls of plants

central nervous system (CNS): the brain and spinal cord

chlorophyll: a green pigment (coloured substance) that absorbs energy from light; the energy is used to combine carbon dioxide with water and make glucose

chromosome: a length of DNA, found in the nucleus of a cell; it contains genetic information in the form of many different genes

ciliary muscle: a circle of muscle surrounding the lens, and joined to it by the suspensory ligaments; when it contracts, it slackens the ligaments so that the lens becomes fatter

circulatory system: a system of blood vessels with a pump and valves to ensure one-way flow of blood

clone: make an identical copy of something

community: all of the populations of all the different species in an ecosystem

complementary: with a perfect mirror-image shape

complementary base pairing: the way in which the bases of the two strands of DNA pair up; A always pairs with T, and C with G

concentration gradient: an imaginary 'slope' from a high concentration to a low concentration

continuous variation: variation in which there is a continuous range of phenotypes between two extremes

cornea: a transparent layer near the front of the eye, which refracts light rays entering the eye

cross-pollination: the transfer of pollen grains from the anther of a flower to the stigma of a flower on a different plant of the same species

cuticle: a thin layer of wax that covers the upper surface of a leaf

cytoplasm: the jelly-like material that fills a cell

DCPIP: a purple liquid that becomes colourless when mixed with vitamin C

death phase: the final stage in a population growth curve where the population falls; death rate exceeds birth rate

deoxygenated blood: blood containing only a little oxygen

dependent variable: the variable that you measure, as you collect your results

diaphragm: a muscle that separates the chest cavity from the abdominal cavity in mammals; it helps with breathing

dichotomous key: a way of identifying an organism, by working through pairs of statements that lead you to its name

dicotyledons: plants with two cotyledons in their seeds

diet: the food eaten in one day

diffusion: the net movement of particles from a region of their higher concentration to a region of their lower concentration (i.e. down a concentration gradient), as a result of their random movement

digestion: the breakdown of food

diploid: having two complete sets of chromosomes

discontinuous variation: variation in which there are distinct categories of phenotype, with no intermediates

DNA: a molecule that contains genetic information, in the form of genes, that controls the proteins that are made in the cell

DNA ligase: an enzyme that joins two DNA molecules together

dominant allele: an allele that is expressed if it is present (e.g. **G**)

double circulatory system: a system in which blood passes through the heart twice on one complete circuit of the body

duodenum: the first part of the small intestine, into which the pancreatic duct and bile duct empty fluids

ecosystem: a unit containing all of the organisms in a community and their environment, interacting together

emulsion: a liquid containing two substances that do not fully mix; one of them forms tiny droplets dispersed throughout the other

enamel: the very strong material that covers the surface of a tooth

endocrine glands: glands that secrete hormones

enzyme–substrate complex: the short-lived structure formed as the substrate binds temporarily to the active site of an enzyme

enzymes: proteins that are involved in all metabolic reactions, where they function as biological catalysts

excretion: the removal of the waste products of metabolism and substances in excess of requirements

exoskeleton: a supportive structure on the outside of the body

expressed: used to make a protein; a gene is expressed when the protein that it codes for is synthesised in a cell

fats: lipids that are solid at room temperature

fermenter: a vessel, usually made of steel or glass, in which microorganisms can be grown in order to produce a required product

fertilisation: the fusion of the nuclei of two gametes

fetus: an unborn mammal, in which all the organs have been formed

food chain: a diagram showing the transfer of energy from one organism to the next, beginning with a producer

food web: a network of interconnected food chains

fully permeable: allows all molecules and ions to pass through it

fungus: an organism whose cells have cell walls, but that does not photosynthesise

gall bladder: a small organ that stores bile, before the bile is released into the duodenum

gamete: a sex cell; a cell with half the normal number of chromosomes, whose nucleus fuses with the nucleus of another gamete during sexual reproduction

gas exchange: the diffusion of oxygen and carbon dioxide into and out of an organism's body

gas exchange surface: a part of the body where gas exchange between the body and the environment takes place

gene: a length of DNA that codes for one protein

genetic diagram: a standard way of showing all the steps in making predictions about the probable genotypes and phenotypes of the offspring from two parents

genetic modification: changing the genetic material of an organism by removing, changing or inserting individual genes

genotype: the genetic makeup of an organism in terms of the alleles present (e.g. **GG**)

genus: a group of species that share similar features and a common ancestor

glucose: a sugar that is used in respiration to release energy

glycogen: a carbohydrate that is used as an energy store in animal cells

gravitropism: a response in which part of a plant grows towards or away from gravity

growth: a permanent increase in size and dry mass

haemoglobin: a red pigment found in red blood cells, which can combine reversibly with oxygen; it is a protein

haploid: having only a single set of chromosomes

heterozygous: having two different alleles of a particular gene (e.g. **Gg**)

high water potential: an area where there are a lot of water molecules – a dilute solution

homozygous: having two identical alleles of a particular gene (e.g. **GG** or **gg**)

hormones: chemicals that are produced by a gland and carried in the blood, which alter the activities of their specific target organs

hydrophyte: a plant that has adaptive features that help it to survive in water

hyphae: microscopic threads, made of cells linked in a long line, that make up the body of a fungus

immune response: the reaction of the body to the presence of an antigen; it involves the production of antibodies

independent variable: the variable that you change in an experiment

insulin: a hormone secreted by the pancreas, which decreases blood glucose concentration

iodine solution: a solution of iodine in potassium iodide; it is orange-brown, and turns blue-black when mixed with starch

iris: the coloured part of the eye; it contains muscles that can alter the size of the pupil

iris reflex (pupil reflex): an automatic response to a change in light intensity; the receptors are in the retina, and the effector is the muscles in the iris

kinetic energy: energy of moving objects

kingdom: one of the major groups into which all organisms are classified

lag phase: the stage at the start of a population growth curve where the population remains small and grows only very slowly

lens: a transparent structure in the eye, which changes shape to focus light rays onto the retina

lignin: a hard, strong, waterproof substance that forms the walls of xylem vessels

limiting factor: a factor that is in short supply, which stops an activity (such as photosynthesis) happening at a faster rate

lipids: substances containing carbon, hydrogen and oxygen; they are insoluble in water and are used as energy stores in organisms

log phase or **exponential phase:** the stage in a population growth curve where the population grows at its maximum rate; birth rate exceeds death rate

low water potential: an area where there are not many water molecules – a concentrated solution

magnification: how many times larger an image is than the actual object

maltase: an enzyme that catalyses the breakdown of maltose to glucose

maltose: a reducing sugar made of two glucose molecules joined together

mammary glands: organs found only in mammals, which produce milk to feed young

meiosis: division of a diploid nucleus resulting in four genetically different haploid nuclei; this is sometimes called a reduction division

memory cells: long-lived cells produced by the division of lymphocytes that have contacted their antigen; memory cells are able to respond quickly to subsequent contact with the same antigen

messenger RNA (mRNA): a molecule that carries a copy of the information on DNA to a ribosome, to be used to synthesise a protein

metabolic reactions: chemical reactions that take place in living organisms

metamorphosis: changing from a larva with one body form to an adult with a different body form

mitochondrion: a small structure in a cell, where aerobic respiration releases energy from glucose

mitosis: division of a cell nucleus resulting in two genetically identical nuclei (i.e. with the same number and kind of chromosomes as the parent nucleus)

monocotyledons: plants with only one cotyledon in their seeds

motor neurone: a neurone that transmits electrical impulses from the central nervous system to an effector

movement: an action by an organism or part of an organism causing a change of position or place

nectar: a sweet liquid secreted by many insect-pollinated flowers, to attract their pollinators

negative feedback: a mechanism that detects a move away from the set point, and brings about actions that take the value back towards the set point

nerve impulse: an electrical signal that passes rapidly along an axon

net movement: overall or average movement

neurone: a cell that is specialised for conducting electrical impulses rapidly

nitrification: converting ammonium ions to nitrate ions

nitrogen fixation: converting inert nitrogen gas into a more reactive form, such as nitrate ions or ammonia

nucleotides: molecules that are linked together into long chains, to make up a DNA molecule

nucleus: a structure containing DNA in the form of chromosomes

oils: lipids that are liquid at room temperature

optic nerve: the nerve that carries electrical impulses from the retina to the brain

optimum: best; for example, the optimum temperature of an enzyme is the temperature at which its activity is greatest

organism: a living thing

osmosis: the diffusion of water molecules through a partially permeable membrane

osmosis (in terms of water potential): the net movement of water molecules from a region of higher water potential (dilute solution) to a region of lower water potential (concentrated solution) through a partially permeable membrane

oxygenated blood: blood containing a lot of oxygen

palisade mesophyll: the layer of cells immediately beneath the upper epidermis, where most photosynthesis happens

pancreas: a creamy-white organ lying close to the stomach, which secretes pancreatic juice; it also secretes the hormones insulin and glucagon, which are involved in the control of blood glucose concentration

partially permeable: allows some molecules and ions to pass through, but not others

partially permeable membrane: a membrane (very thin layer) that lets some particles move through it, but prevents others passing through

pathogen: a microorganism that causes disease, such as bacteria

pectinase: an enzyme that is used to digest pectin, increasing the quantity of juice that can be extracted from fruit, and clarifying the juice

peripheral nervous system (PNS): the nerves outside the brain and spinal cord

petals: coloured structures that attract insects or birds to a flower

phenotype: the observable features of an organism

phloem: a plant tissue made up of living cells joined end to end; it transports substances made by the plant, such as sucrose and amino acids

photosynthesis: the process by which plants synthesise carbohydrates from raw materials using energy from light

phototropism: a response in which part of a plant grows towards or away from the direction from which light is coming

pinna: a flap on the outside of the body that directs sound into the ear

placenta: an organ that connects the growing fetus to its mother, in which the blood of the fetus and mother are brought close together so that materials can be exchanged between them

plasma: the liquid part of blood

platelets: tiny cell fragments present in blood, which help with clotting

pollen grains: small structures which contain the male gametes of a flower

pollination: the transfer of pollen grains from the male part of the plant (anther of stamen) to the female part of the plant (stigma)

product: the new substance formed by a chemical reaction

protein: a substance whose molecules are made of many amino acids linked together; each different protein has a different sequence of amino acids

pulmonary artery: the artery that carries deoxygenated blood from the right ventricle to the lungs

pulmonary veins: the veins that carry oxygenated blood from the lungs to the left atrium of the heart

pupil: a circular gap in the middle of the iris, through which light can pass

range: the lowest to the highest value

receptors: cells or groups of cells that detect stimuli

recessive allele: an allele that is only expressed when there is no dominant allele of the gene present (e.g. **g**)

recombinant plasmid: a small circle of DNA, found in bacteria, which contains both the bacterial DNA and DNA from a different organism

red blood cells: biconcave blood cells with no nucleus, which transport oxygen

reducing sugars: sugars such as glucose, which turn Benedict's solution orange-red when heated together

relay neurone: a neurone that transmits electrical impulses within the central nervous system

reproduction: the processes that make more of the same kind of organism

respiration: the chemical reactions in cells that break down nutrient molecules and release energy for metabolism

restriction enzymes: enzymes (biological catalysts) that cut DNA at specific points, and leave a short length of unpaired bases at each end

retina: a tissue at the back of the eye that contains receptor cells that respond to light

ribosomes: very small structures in a cell that use information on DNA to make protein molecules

salivary glands: groups of cells close to the mouth, which secrete saliva into the salivary ducts

selection pressure: something in the environment that affects the chance that individuals with different features will survive and reproduce

selective breeding: choosing particular organisms with desired characteristics to breed together, and continuing this over many generations

self-pollination: the transfer of pollen grains from the anther of a flower to the stigma of the same flower, or a different flower on the same plant

sensitivity: the ability to detect and respond to changes in the internal or external environment

sensory neurone: a neurone that transmits electrical impulses from a receptor to the central nervous system

set point: the normal value or range of values for a particular parameter – for example, the normal range of blood glucose concentration or the normal body temperature

sex-linked genes: genes that are found on a part of one of the sex chromosomes (usually the X chromosome) and not on the other sex chromosomes; they therefore produce characteristics that are more common in one sex than in the other

sexual reproduction: a process involving the fusion of two gametes to form a zygote and the production of offspring that are genetically different from each other

sigmoid growth curve: an S-shaped curve showing the change in the size of a population through all the phases in population growth

single circulatory system: a system in which blood passes through the heart only once on one complete circuit of the body

sink: part of a plant to which sucrose or amino acids are being transported, and where they are used or stored

small intestine: a long, narrow part of the alimentary canal, consisting of the duodenum and ileum

source: part of a plant that releases sucrose or amino acids, to be transported to other parts

species: a group of organisms that can reproduce to produce fertile offspring

spongy mesophyll: the layer of cells immediately beneath the palisade mesophyll, where some photosynthesis happens; this tissue contains a lot of air spaces between the cells

spores: very small groups of cells surrounded by a protective wall, used in reproduction

starch: a carbohydrate that is used as an energy store in plant cells

stationary phase: the stage in a population growth curve where the population remains roughly constant; birth rate equals death rate

stem cells: unspecialised cells that are able to divide by mitosis to produce different types of specialised cell

sterilised: treated – e.g. with steam – to destroy all living cells

sticky ends: lengths of unpaired bases on one strand of a DNA molecule; they are able to form bonds with complementary lengths of unpaired bases on a different DNA molecule

stigma: the part of a flower that receives pollen

stimuli (singular: **stimulus**): changes in the environment that can be detected by organisms

stomach: a wide part of the alimentary canal, in which food can be stored for a while, and where the digestion of protein begins

stomata (singular: **stoma**): openings in the surface of a leaf, most commonly in the lower surface; they are surrounded by pairs of guard cells, which control whether the stomata are open or closed

substrate: the substance that an enzyme acts upon

sucrose: a sugar whose molecules are made of glucose and another similar molecule (fructose) linked together

sugars: carbohydrates that have relatively small molecules; they are soluble in water and they taste sweet

suspensory ligaments: strong, inelastic fibres that hold the lens in position; when they are under tension, they pull the lens into a thinner shape

synapse: a junction between two neurones

target organs: organs whose activity is altered by a hormone

transmissible disease: a disease that can be passed from one host to another; transmissible diseases are caused by pathogens

transpiration: the loss of water vapour from leaves

trophic level: the position of an organism in a food chain, food web or ecological pyramid

tropism: a growth response by a plant, in which the direction of growth is related to the direction of the stimulus

type 1 diabetes: a condition in which insufficient insulin is secreted by the pancreas, so that blood glucose concentration is not controlled

urea: a waste product produced in the liver, from the breakdown of excess amino acids

vaccine: a harmless preparation of dead or inactivated pathogens that is injected into the body to induce an immune response

vacuole: a fluid-filled space inside a cell, separated from the cytoplasm by a membrane

valves: structures that allow a liquid to flow in one direction only

vena cava: the large vein that brings deoxygenated blood to the right atrium

ventricles: the thick-walled chambers at the base of the heart, which pump out blood

villi (singular: **villus**): very small finger-like projections that line the inner surface of the small intestine, greatly increasing its surface area

water potential gradient: a difference in water potential between two areas

white blood cells: blood cells with a nucleus, which help to defend against pathogens

xylem: a plant tissue made up of dead, empty cells joined end to end; it transports water and mineral ions and helps to support the plant

zygote: a cell that is formed by the fusion of two gametes

Acknowledgements

The authors and publishers acknowledge the following sources of copyright material and are grateful for the permissions granted.
While every effort has been made, it has not always been possible to identify the sources of all the material used, or to trace all copyright holders.
If any omissions are brought to our notice, we will be happy to include the appropriate acknowledgements on reprinting.

Thanks to the following for permission to reproduce images:

dem10/Getty Images; SCIEPRO/SCIENCE PHOTO LIBRARY/Getty Images; goldhafen/Getty Images; alxpin/Getty Images; Difydave/Getty Images; Roland Magnusson / EyeEm/Getty Images Eleanor Jones/Getty Images; ThomasVogel/Getty Images; Anton Novoderezhkin/Getty Images JGalione/Getty Images; twomeows/Getty Images; S. Greg Panosian/Getty Images; Indeed/Getty Images; Ixefra/Getty Images; KATERYNA KON/SCIENCE PHOTO LIBRARY/Getty Images; LockieCurrie/Getty Images; Richard Bailey/ Getty Images; Kaveh Kazemi/Getty Images; Margie Politzer/Getty Images; Maskot/Getty Images; Eraxion/Getty Images; SEBASTIAN KAULITZKI/SCIENCE PHOTO LIBRARY/Getty Images; Peter Cade/Getty Images; Ger Bosma/Getty Images